P U B W
──────O N──────
The Isle Of Wight

THIRTY CIRCULAR WALKS
AROUND
ISLE OF WIGHT INNS

John Hague

COUNTRYSIDE BOOKS
NEWBURY, BERKSHIRE

COUNTRYSIDE BOOKS
3 Catherine Road
Newbury, Berkshire

ISBN 1 85306 242 1

Publisher's Note

We hope that you obtain considerable enjoyment from this book; great care has been taken in its preparation. However, changes of landlord and actual closures are sadly not uncommon. We are anxious that all details concerning both pubs and walks are kept as up to date as possible, and would therefore welcome information from readers which would be relevant to future editions.

Designed by Mon Mohan
Cover illustration by Colin Doggett
Photographs and maps by the author

Produced through MRM Associates Ltd., Reading
Typeset by Paragon Typesetters, Queensferry, Clwyd
Printed in England

To my wife Jennifer for all her help.

Contents

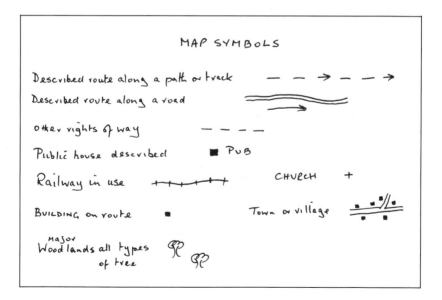

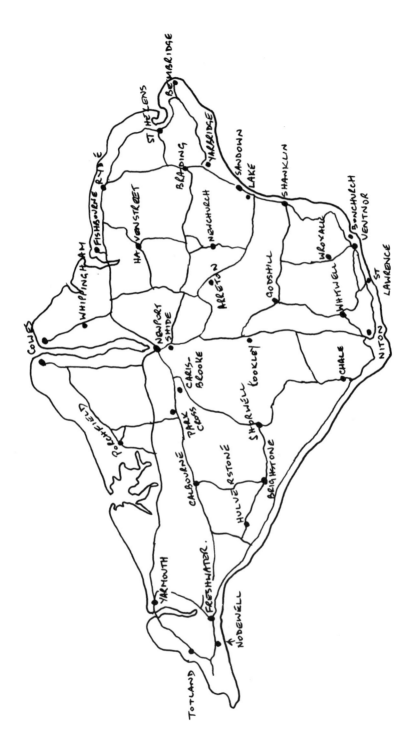

Area map showing locations of the walks.

Introduction

Welcome to Insula Vectis. It is impossible to move far on the island without noticing the liberal use of the Roman name for Wight – indeed travel is by Southern Vectis buses. The island passed through history in much the same way as mainland Britain, to which it was once joined. The effects of invaders remain and the island is proud of its history. Today it battles, as do others, to maintain an economic structure but one which is orientated towards tourists and visitors.

As you use this book, walk the paths and visit the pubs, do talk to those whom you may meet. You will find them exceedingly helpful and friendly, and those who are true islanders will have a depth of knowledge of the countryside they are pleased to impart. We 'overners' will never become islanders however long we remain, but there is generally a village spirit encompassing the whole island. I was received by all in a welcoming manner and most of the information in this book was from local people.

The paths I have used on these walks you will find in the main to be in excellent condition and well used. The County Council, parish councils, Ramblers' Association and other volunteers work hard to maintain the standard. I am sure you will find the routes easy to follow but it would be useful if any obstructions or problems are notified to the County Council. I have tried to select walks which pass through a variety of areas. The downs and the coasts are obviously the most spectacular with regard to views but the inland field walks should not be neglected. They can be particularly revealing of hidden parts of the land and history of the island. Some of the walks just had to go in as the best – in my opinion – on the island. If you use an Ordnance Survey map (sheet 29 of the Outdoor Leisure series covers the island) you may notice that occasionally my described route differs from the map. Don't worry – stick to the written word. Some of the map paths have now changed and in some instances the path on the ground follows a slightly more convenient route. Convenient, that is, to both walker and landowner, who have allowed a slight change by common consent. All the paths used are either definitive or permissive (which I have indicated).

Pubs on the island – like the roads – are different (but I can't explain why)! Those I have included in this book have all been chosen not only because they suit a walk, but because they are attractive as a hostelry. From the many pubs on the island I had to choose 30 – an almost impossible task in some districts.

Landlords change and so therefore does the food and drink – but never to a great extent. All the pubs in the book serve good food and I found many varied menus, extracts from which are in each chapter. The walker must try them to find all that is on offer. Generally you may not eat your own food, even in the garden, and the walker must respect this. However most menus have inexpensive items on offer so it should be no hardship. Less weight to carry in the rucksack!

Opening hours were tricky to itemise. The times I have included were the general ones adhered to by each pub, but the indication often was that the landlord varied them according to the day's trade. In summer the hours are often more extensive. Sundays were always 12 noon to 3 pm and 7 pm to 10.30 pm – thus the note about 'restricted' times in each section.

Like most people, the landlords welcome walkers but not muddy boots so it would be nice if they were left outside. You should find that on most of the walks you won't get a lot of mud – but I can't guarantee that. Similarly with dogs. On the walks the landowners are most insistent that dogs should not be allowed to roam – there are a lot of sheep and cattle about. All the landlords were pleased to allow them in the pub but a wet muddy dog won't be popular. Children are usually welcome in pubs these days and there are often special rooms for them. I did notice that landlords prefer the youngsters to use these rooms – but if they are full do ask. I am sure they will try to accommodate.

I have included bus details in each chapter. You will find summer services are more extensive. Do check beforehand as some of the routes listed are quite infrequent. The island bus timetable is great value.

I trust you will have as much enjoyment from reading and using this book as I had in preparing it for you. If you haven't visited the island recently, or ever before, perhaps the thought of such good walks, food and drink will encourage you to come. If you already reside on the island the book may help you to discover new walks and pubs. Once here you will, I am sure, come back time and time again to visit this unique garden isle. Our Insula Vectis.

John Hague
Spring 1993

① Totland
The Broadway Inn

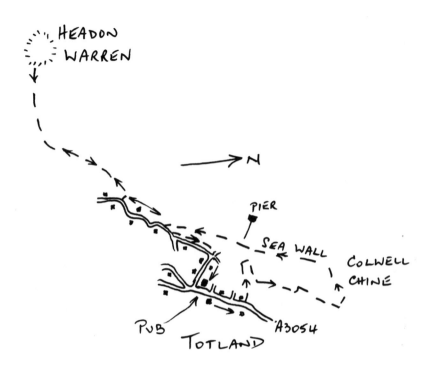

Although it has been a pub for only some 40 years the Broadway characterises its Victorian origins both inside and out. Formerly a grocer's shop, it has been pictured with the great cannons that were transported to the Needles Battery (a defensive fort) and shown resting outside on their journey. A friendly welcome invites the visitor to partake of a variety of homecooked foods. Steak and kidney pies are popular and vegetarians have a choice of dishes. I had a particularly good ploughman's with generous portions. The real ales are Boddingtons, Flowers and Eldridge Pope Royal Oak, a good selection for all tastes. Low cost doubles are a feature of the extensive spirits list.

Children are not forgotten – they are welcome at all times, but the visitor with a dog should ask the landlord if the bar is clear of competing canines. Should the weather be kind there is a paved patio at the side on which to rest and relax, and if you have your own sandwiches with you, you may eat them there with your purchased drinks. The opening hours are 11.30 am to 3 pm and 6 pm to 11 pm, but all day on Saturday and the usual restricted hours on Sunday. Live music on Thursday and Saturday evenings provides entertainment and the aroma of the summer barbecue will guide the walker back to the right place. Accommodation is available.

A visit here will complement the walk and who knows, you may be lucky enough to hear the ghost of the long gone 'chippie' who worked in the carpenter's yard at the back.

Telephone: 0983 752453.

How to get there: The pub is in the cente of Totland on the Yarmouth to Alum Bay road. It stands on the corner of the turning to the beach at the roundabout. Southern Vectis buses 1B, 1C, 7, 7A from Ryde, Newport, Yarmouth and Alum Bay (Sandown and Shanklin, summer only).

Parking: There is no pub car park but just before the roundabout on the left from Yarmouth is a free public car park.

Length of the walk: 3¾ miles.

An easy walk to Colwell Chine along an enclosed path, followed by a sea wall return to the pier. From the pier the way climbs onto Headon Warren where one can vary the distance at will. Extensive views and, in rough weather, an exciting coast section.

The Walk
Leave the public car park, cross the road and turn right along the main street past the shops. Walk past two side roads on the left, and after a further 100 yards turn left down a rough lane to public conveniences. Continue down the gravelled path with a recreation area on the right to join a tarmac path straight on in front of the houses. Proceed straight on and note the former coastguard station on the right. Just past this, turn sharp right up steps with a railing to follow the path leading forward between hedges which sometimes join overhead. In a short while the main path turns sharp left on a gravelly surface – not straight on into the football field. Follow the main path with a scrub area on the left. Continue forward at any junctions on a winding path between hedges to cross a tarmac road leading to Fort Warden. Fingerpost – Colwell Bay. Continue forward on the tarmac path to join the road and turn left to the sea front at Colwell Chine. Cafés and toilets are available in season.

At the water's edge turn left along the top of the sea wall but at high tides with very high waves, do have some caution near the edge. Walk along the wall to Totland pier (now disused) with views to the mainland and Hurst Castle, Fort Albert behind you along the coast (an unusual block building of wartime sea defence origins) and a surprise

11

view of the Needles as you round the point. From the pier continue on the sea wall to its end at the old lifeboat station and note the old Totland Tide Tables on a board on the side wall. Just past the lifeboat station turn left up the steps with railings and continue climbing from the steps up a short track to the road. Turn right up the road for about ¼ mile and where the road curves left take a path to the right towards the cliffs – fingerpost Alum Bay. Follow the path behind houses and enter the National Trust area of Headon Warren. Walk gently uphill through a wooded area to exit onto open ground. Take the left fork at a wooden post to follow the coast path upwards. After about 100 yards the next post points to the right. Follow this direction uphill to the top of Headon Warren. You will see the ancient barrows with an explanatory board and the area can be walked round outside the rails.

At this point the walk returns downhill after taking in the extensive views, but if you wish you may follow the path further along the ridge of the Warren to see the view of Alum Bay and the Needles. You should, however, eventually walk back to the explanatory board to follow the return directions.

From the board follow the posts down over the same route – bearing left at the first post and slightly right at the second to take the exit path through the wooded area back to the road. Turn left down the road and continue past the path you came up from the lifeboat station. After a few hundred yards a wide grassy strip, known as the Turf Walk, opens up before you on the left of the road.

The early holidaymakers had the choice of two types of strolling areas – the 'Sea Walk' with the pier and the 'Turf Walk', and one can imagine the Victorians gently taking the air.

Walk along the Turf Walk and shortly before it finishes rejoin the road for a few yards to the crossroads. Turn right towards Totland and a short walk brings you to the Broadway Inn. The public car park is reached by turning left and crossing the road.

This walk could be divided into two shorter walks, with refreshments at the pub in between. The road you have walked up from the crossroads comes up from the pier as a narrow tarmac lane.

② Nodewell
The Highdown Inn

Built in the early 1800s, this comfortable pub, with its unusually plain exterior, was only a beer house until 1931 when it obtained a full licence. Situated close under the downs, it would have been named from Highdown Lane which passed the side of the pub to reach the Highdown Cliffs and the Downs above. This is Tennyson country, and he wandered the lanes, paths and downs nearby. Undoubtedly the closeness of Farringford House to the inn would have resulted in a visit during one of his sojourns on the downs.

Inside, good home cooking is on the menu (the fish dishes are particularly delicious) and children are welcome but need to be kept tucked away. The two rooms are cosy and compact, and the bar serves an excellent pint. Now an Ushers pub, the real ales of Best Bitter and Founders make a good drink. Normal pub opening hours are kept with Sunday restrictions. Overnight accommodation is available and this quiet location is ideal for local walks. Well behaved dogs are allowed in but space is restricted.

Telephone: 0983 752450.

How to get there: The pub is reached by the minor road from Freshwater Bay to Alum Bay – close under the Downs. It is on the left coming from Freshwater Bay on a sharp right corner. Nearest buses are at Freshwater Bay, Totland, and Alum Bay.

Parking: There is a pub car park just inside the lane to the left – or a few yards up at the end of the lane a chalk pit has space for cars. Customers may leave their cars in the pub car park whilst they walk but please ask the landlord first.

Length of the walk: 3 ¾ miles.

A reasonably level walk towards Alum Bay followed by a climb onto West High Down and to Tennyson's Monument. A visit to Alum Bay Leisure Park and the Needles Old Battery can be incorporated. Spectacular views in all directions and an opportunity to see the coloured cliffs from which the sand is extracted.

The Walk
Follow the track from the pub to the entrance to the chalk pit and turn right below the downs. Cross the stile at the end of the track by Nodes Beacon (see explanatory plate) and take the right hand path going slightly down, fingerpost Alum Bay. Continue forward following a line of electricity wires with the Alum Bay complex coming into view on the right, to reach a stile to the right of a small brick blockhouse. Join a tarmac lane. Alum Bay Leisure Complex (café and toilets in season) can be reached by turning right as also can the beach. However the walk turns left along the lane – but take the opportunity to walk on the high verge for the views of the bay and the famous coloured cliffs below. Despite the amount sold in souvenirs there is still a lot of colour remaining.

After about ¼ mile bear left up some steps and over a stile to follow a well worn path ascending slightly right over the brow. Note the coastguard cottages on the left, but cross the stile in front to join a tarmac lane and turn left. In the area on the right hand side of the lane are the Needles Batteries, and the site of the rocket testing station, used after the war for the testing of Britain's first rocket propulsion units (for the Black Knight). If you have time, explore the area. There are explanatory boards, view points and a lot of history. Needles Old Battery is a National Trust property with an entrance charge.

The walk continues up the lane – which bends sharply left at a brick building. Just after this bend bear slightly right to pass a wireless mast on your right and the cottages on the left. Cross a stile with a gate at the side and continue forward heading generally for Tennyson's Monument on the skyline. Keep to the high part of the ridge with

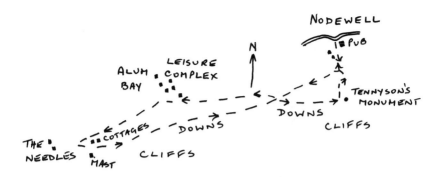

views down the 'Back of the Wight' with the rocky outcrop of Blackgang in the far distance and St Catherine's lighthouse a white blob underneath.

The top of West High Down is reached, marked by a small stone post and the walk continues forward along the ridge, generally towards Tennyson's Monument. Across the Solent to the left can be seen Hurst Castle situated at the end of a long shingle bank, used formerly as a defensive fort for the entrance to the Solent. The navigation channel here is very narrow and the water runs fast and treacherously. In this area many vessels were lost and surveyors are considering raising some of the remains. The path now goes slightly further to the left of the ridge and then passes through an area of gorse to reach again the gate and stile at Nodes Beacon. Cross the stile and bear right – fingerpost Tennyson Down, Freshwater Bay, Coastal Path. Climb directly to Tennyson's Monument, a high spot from which the Spanish Armada was sighted in 1588. At this point a County Council leafleted walk called the Tennyson Trail starts. This follows the high downs to Carisbrooke near Newport.

To find the path back to the pub – stand with your back to the monument and the cliffs and walk directly away from the open sea, with Hurst Castle and lighthouse in front, towards an area of trees and gorse. You will see a well worn path in front of you which should be followed down – with occasional steps. The path skirts the edge of the chalk pit to your left and then turns sharp left down into it. A board explains West High Down. Walk out of the chalk pit by the vehicle track and keep straight down the lane to the pub.

3 Freshwater
The Red Lion

This pub is an unexpected find in a corner of Freshwater away from the bustling town. I discovered it whilst walking the Freshwater Way and was immediately struck by its village pub atmosphere and its characteristic position by the church, flanked by cottages. The history of the Red Lion is varied and is linked with the Norman church which stands close by. Three generations of the Tennyson family rest in the churchyard and the church itself is very worthy of a visit. There seems to have been a group of ecclesiastical buildings close to the church, one of them a refectory. This then became the public house in the early 1700s, a thatched property. Reports of a friendly ghost who opens doors and taps on floors would seem to strengthen the connections with its former occupants. In more recent times a landlord proved to be a local character, with a large collection of hats of all shapes, sizes and descriptions on view.

Today there is a friendly welcome to a comfortable roomy interior. Original flagstone floors and exposed brickwork and beams retain the character, and a variety of liquid refreshments include real ale of Flowers, Marston's Pedigree and Eldridge Pope Royal Oak with draught cider from Taunton Dry. The separate room areas are all

16

served from one open bar and children are welcome in the end away from the bar. An extensive menu offers a choice of hot meals and cold snacks with plenty of home-cooked food. Choose from fish dishes and grills, and see what the special is on the day. Should the weather be kind the large rear garden is available and pretty flower beds make attractive surroundings. The opening hours are normal pub hours with restricted times on Sunday. If you have your canine friend with you he can accompany you inside.

Telephone: 0983 754925.

How to get there: The Red Lion is not in Freshwater main centre. From Yarmouth take the first turn left off the A3054, the Totland road. Just after entering the village outskirts the main road turns sharp right with a shop on the corner. Turn left for the pub. From Freshwater Bay follow signs for Yarmouth to reach the sharp left corner on the A3055. Drive straight on to the pub. Buses 1B, 1C, 7, 7A pass close by from Yarmouth, Newport and Ryde.

Parking: The pub car park at the side is not large but if you find a space you may leave your car there while you walk. The roadway parking is also limited especially as church parking occupies the road as well. Visitors may wish to consider parking in Yarmouth, which is also easier for bus travel, and walking, making the Red Lion a halfway stopping point.

Length of the walk: 3¾ miles.

A level walk throughout, offering views of the Yar estuary with occasional distant glimpses of the downs. An opportunity to visit Yarmouth is included. This walk can be a paradise for those keen on seashore bird watching as the salt marshes are extensive.

The Walk

Leave the Red Lion and turn left to the church gate and immediately left down the outside of the churchyard wall. Fingerpost Yarmouth/ Freshwater Way. The Freshwater Way is a County Council leaflet route from Freshwater Bay to Yarmouth and the walk follows it to Yarmouth.

The enclosed path crosses two stiles to join the end of a lane. Continue forward along the lane with views to the right across the river Yar. The lane approaches Kings Manor Farm and, at the point where the lane becomes concrete and passes through the farm gateway, turn sharp left over a double stile into the field – fingerpost Yarmouth.

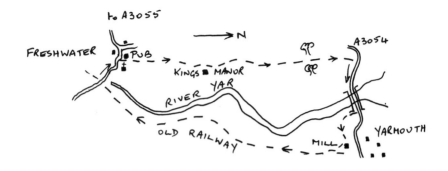

In the field turn right and follow the line of the edge of the field some 10 to 20 yards from it. Continue forward past farm buildings, noting the electricity pylon with path direction arms attached. Immediately in front is the stile to enter an enclosed path to exit onto a track at a metal kissing gate. Turn half left towards a stile at the side of a gate and note the main drive to Kings Manor crossing the path from left to right. Cross the stile and continue along the track with the hedge on the right for 1½ fields and then turn right across the field on the same track. Yarmouth can just be seen in the distance to the right. The track continues, sloping down towards a spinney. At the point where it enters, a stile can be seen on the right – fingerpost Yarmouth. Cross the stile and plank bridge, walk through the spinney and exit over another bridge and stile into field. Turn left and follow the edge round until the spinney turns sharply away left. Cross the stile forwards and follow the path with a wire fence on the right. The path makes its way towards the next spinney and a white fingerpost – Main Road Yarmouth. Cross the stile and walk along the edge of the spinney with a wire fence on the right. The path then drops sharply to exit onto a lane through a stagger gate. Turn left along the lane to join the main Yarmouth to Totland road, turning right towards Yarmouth and crossing the river Yar on the swing bridge. This bridge opens for river traffic to allow the passage of high-masted vessels.

Immediately after crossing the bridge, turn right along the tarmac path at the edge of the water and green area. Note to your left a piece of timber mounted on a plinth. This is a bit of the original timber Yar bridge in use until replaced by the present bridge in 1987. Follow the tarmac path to the boat park, turning left along the edge and then right between the car park and boat park to reach a further tarmac path and interpretation board about the Yar estuary.

At this point you may well decide to visit Yarmouth centre, a worthwhile diversion. The quay and marina have interesting craft and the lifeboat, whilst the town has a castle (open to the public), ancient coaching inns and narrow streets. To reach the town, cross the car park and main road and head for the church, but be sure to note your way in order to return to this point to continue your walk.

The walk continues along the tarmac path at the water's edge towards the mill. At the end of the tarmac turn right along the track. The tidemill principle was to allow the rising tide to fill a pool or tidal area, in this case the Thorley brook and its upstream ponds, and at high water the gates could be closed and the captured water released at will to drive machinery. Continue straight on across the causeway. At the far end pass through concrete posts and turn right along the former railway track, the extension of the Newport to Yarmouth line which ran to Freshwater.

Walk along the track for some 1¾ miles, a pleasant stroll through wooded areas. Turn and look back for a fine view of the spread of Yarmouth town and its church. The view forward and right is of Tennyson Down and the monument is just visible on top, whilst to the left the land opens up to show the distant downs of Bowcombe and Newbarn with Rowridge television transmitter on the skyline. Eventually the track reaches the road with Freshwater church standing high to the right. Turn right along the road over the bridge and causeway to return up the hill to the Red Lion.

Hulverstone
The Sun Inn

Hulverstone is a tiny hamlet but boasts an attractive pub. Now catering more for visitors, some 600 years ago when it was built it must have relied on locals and workers from the scattered farms and estates. The thatched building looks most attractive in summer with window boxes and tubs and a large garden area which has won an award for its flowers and attractive layout. Tales of smuggling abound and even rumour of a tunnel from the pub towards the coast. I think the filled-in archway in the pub back was more likely a below ground store!

The landlord and his wife run the pub together; he deals with the liquid refreshment whilst his wife cooks. She specialises in steak and kidney pie, ever popular, and a good beef curry. There is a wide selection and I am told fresh local caught lobster is well known in season. Also try the ploughman's for a hungry lunchtime. The drink side is extensive. A George Gale pub, the two real ale bitters, HSB and Best, are a good pint whilst cider drinkers can choose from Dry Blackthorn and Scrumpy Jack. If you like country wines then this is the pub to try them. They can be purchased by the glass but if you wish to take them home there are bottles for sale, in which case you can have a wine taste in order to make your selection. With the full range of 20 different country wines the decision will not be easy. There is also a very wide range of spirits.

The bar area is a single room with no family area, so children are not allowed in the pub itself, however they can go in the garden and there is a chalet outside for inclement summer days. Occasionally there are barbecues and groups may be able to use the barbecue area for themselves by prior contact with the landlord. The opening times are 11 am to 3.30 pm and 6 pm to 11 pm with the usual Sunday restrictions.

Telephone: 0983 740403.

How to get there: Hulverstone is on the B3399 Freshwater Bay to Chale inland road and just off the Military Road (coast route) north east of Brook. Southern Vectis bus 1B Newport to Freshwater service.

Parking: There is a large car park. The landlord would like to know if you are leaving your car there while you walk.

Length of the walk: 3¾ miles.

A variety of landscapes is the feature of this walk. A flat easy walk along the cliffs is followed by a climb onto the edge of the downs and a stroll through pleasant woodland.

The Walk
Leave the pub, turn left a few yards along the road and then left down the outside of the pub garden, fingerposted public footpath. Follow the edge of the field with hedge and wire on the left. As the path curves right another path can be seen parallel on the other side of the fence and ditch. When the ditch becomes open and level with the pond on the left, look for a plank bridge across the ditch. Cross the bridge, ignoring waymarks pointing right. On the other side turn right and continue down between ditch and pond. Cross the stile, then go forward following electricity wires and cross another stile. A few yards after the electricity wires turn away right, look for a stile in front in the corner. Cross into an enclosed path past a cottage on the left. Go over the stile into the driveway and walk to the right – fingerpost Brook Village. Leave the drive at the road in the village.

A reading room, established here by Sir Charles Seely, was the forerunner of the County Library Service. Directly as a result of his enthusiasm and financial help a combined library and centre for technical education was built. This prospered and grew to the present islandwide library that bears his name and the College of Arts and Technology. Turn right to look at the village. The route turns left

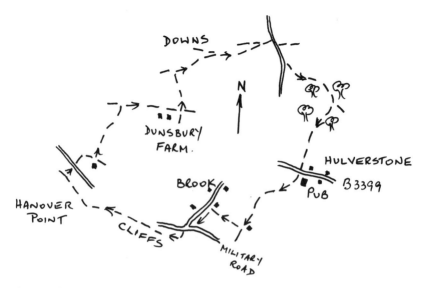

down the lane to the Military Road and crosses into Brook Chine (National Trust). Sir Charles Seely features here too, in that as a result of his beneficence the first Brook lifeboat was launched in 1860. Smuggling also returns to mind and stories tell of smuggling runs around this part of the coast. The isolated row of cottages, some with thatch, have a pleasant outlook on summer days, but it's very different on stormy winter nights with high seas running. The lifeboat was housed here, as was the local coastguard.

Walk along the track a few yards and then bear right onto the grass as the track starts to slope down. Keep on the grass – with the chine on the left – and head for the car park. Cross the stile, go through the gate and turn left past the information board which has interesting aspects of this area. Turn left again along the edge of the car park and leave by a stile onto the coast path. Follow the coast away from Brook Chine with views of Freshwater Bay and Tennyson Down to the front. In a while the path rounds a point jutting out slightly from the cliff and raised. This is Hanover Point and immediately out to sea is a tower or sea mark. Just below the cliff, on the shore, are several large rocks. These are fossilised parts of dinosaurs – I have seen two footprints and a vertebra. They are quite distinctive shapes, the footprints showing three toes and the footpad in positive relief. Too large to miss, or remove, they sit at the high water mark and can be visited along the shore at times below high tide.

Continue along the cliff a few hundred yards and view the shoreline again. At very low tides a fossilised forest of pine rafts is visible. These are logs of fallen trees lying in the sea and the distinctive shape and

22

texture of pines can be clearly seen in rock form. Continue along to the car park at Shippards Chine, with access to the shore and a well known surfing beach. Turn right across to the toilets and road, then left along the road and cross over to the track – fingerpost Brook and The Downs.

Walk along the track to the cottage and turn left up a grass track – fingerpost Dunsbury Farm and The Downs. Follow the edge of the field with a ditch on the left, uphill. Pass to the right of the copse on the track and go up to the junction at the top edge. This area of copse was formerly a withy bed where the supple shoots were collected to make lobster pots and baskets. Turn right along the track which comes along the top of the copse and continue to Dunsbury Farm. On the skyline in front can be seen Brook Hill House, now luxury flats. Pass the farm buildings, ignoring a fingerpost to the right. A few yards further turn left, fingerposted Brook Down, and follow the route uphill between hedges. Continue forward until a track rises from the right and a junction is reached a few yards further on.

Turn right, fingerposted public bridleway. This is part of the Hamstead Trail – a County Council waymarked route from south to north coast. Go along the track with woodland on the right and downs to the left. Soon another track rises from the valley on the left and the route joins this to bear right along it. Continue, now downhill, along the general line of the electricity wires. From here there are views to the right along the coast as far as the distinctive bluff at Blackgang.

Go forward, joining another track from the left and then pass through a gate and down on a firmer surface to the road. Turn right, ignoring the track almost opposite. After some 200 yards bear left along a drive which appears to be a private entrance. It is! To Brook Hill House. However, the footpath sign 'The Longstone, Strawberry Lane, Mottistone' reassures the walker. Follow the drive along to the orchard and when it curves right, keep slightly left along a woodland track with a loose fingerboard repeating the direction. This track curves left and just before a stile take a path to the right sharply down through the trees. The sign at the side says 'Private woodland – please keep to the path'. Do not continue forward over the stile into Forestry Commission land, but follow the winding path down through young beech, then conifers, then beech again to a stile into open field. Cross the field forward in the curved bottom and pass under the wires about halfway between poles. At the fence line in front, a stile and gate pass into the next field. Go down this with the hedge on the left. At the next fence cross over the stile into an enclosed path which exits onto the road opposite the pub.

⑤ Calbourne
The Sun Inn

The name of the inn seems to originate from Sun Hill, the raised field across the junction – or vice versa! It was built about 100 years ago as a Mew Langton pub and you can have a look at a copy of the original lease on the bar. The earlier building was burnt down and the present one was a combined pub and farm until about 1950. Mains water being a later village acquisition, the original pub well was over by the sports field, and the village pump is on the church green under its own roof. The main road has been re-routed to the other side of the building, its earlier direction being through the present car park.

Inside, the pub is large, comfortable and welcoming. An extension on the rear provides a dining room, which is a no smoking area and also caters for children. There is an extensive selection of food to choose from, with homemade specials and a roast lunch on Sundays. The fish meals are particularly good. The Sun is a freehouse and serves an excellent Courage pint, both Best Bitter and Directors. Outside, a patio and garden provide a pleasant area during better weather. Pub hours here are 11 am to 3 pm, 6 pm to 11 pm and possibly all day Saturday. Sunday hours are the usual restricted ones.

Telephone: 0983 78231.

How to get there: The Sun Inn is on the B3401 Carisbrooke to Yarmouth road at Calbourne crossroads. Buses 1C, 7A and 36 serve Calbourne from Yarmouth, Newport and Ryde.

Parking: The pub car park is reputedly the largest in West Wight, but ask the landlord for permission to leave your car there while you walk. Alternatively you could park in the car park mentioned in the walk. This is on the Brighstone to Calbourne road, right on top of the pass over the downs. The walk could then incorporate the pub halfway.

Length of the walk: 4¾ miles.

The walks starts with the village and rural fields and then negotiates woodland whilst climbing steadily to the top of the down. The effort of the climb is well rewarded by the views and the return is partly down a pleasantly wooded lane.

The Walk

Cross the main road and go down the road opposite, to the village. On your left on the church green is the village pump house. At the bottom of the sloping street bear right into Barrington Row, known locally as Winkle Street. One theory is that the name comes from a freshwater snail formerly found in the stream or Caul Bourne. Walk along Winkle Street, an attractive row of stone cottages with pretty gardens and a watercress filled stream. Note the facility in the stream for damming it, to form a sheep dip. Pop into the artist's cottage part way along and view her interesting paintings.

At the end of the cottages continue down a path to a gate and stile. In the field turn left over the footbridge and stile. Continue forward across the field to a double stile and then across to another double stile in a wire fence. Cross and continue forward between wire fences heading for the wooded downs in front. At the end of the enclosed path cross a double stile and continue forward, but slightly right, down to woods. Cross the stile in the hedge and enter woods over a footbridge. Follow the winding path forward to leave the woods by a stile onto a track. Turn right along the track down and up to Westover Farm buildings. Keep straight on with the main buildings to your left and ignoring the track on the right. The track bends left soon and is accompanied by a hedge on the right. It then becomes grassy and goes straight up to the woodland. Do not change hedge sides. Looking back now gives a view over the Solent to the mainland. It is interesting what a small increase in height can reveal.

Enter the woodland on a track which immediately turns right to follow the inside edge of the wood, starting to climb and swinging to the left in a large gentle curve. Go uphill to a track crossing left to right

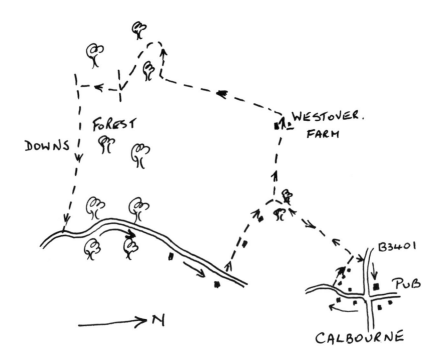

and go straight over, up to a multiple junction. At this point bear left on a wider, level track and continue to a more complicated junction in an open area, but stop just on the edge of this open space. A straight track comes from behind on your right and continues across the open area, but this is not the route in either direction. Almost straight across is another wide track leading away from you. Go over and enter this and then immediately bear right on a smaller track going uphill fairly steeply. Follow this to the top and pass through a bridle gate. Three paces forward brings you onto a left/right track on the top of Mottistone Down. Down immediately in front, but hidden from view, is the ancient manor of Mottistone, home of the county's Lord Lieutenant and now Governor of the Island. Look left and the view along the coast is outstanding. The distant bluff is Gore Cliff, over-shadowing Blackgang Chine.

Turn left and follow the track down. This is now the Tennyson Trail to Carisbrooke. The view forward is of Brighstone Down and the village nestles at the bottom on the right. Pass through the car park onto the road and turn left. Walk down the road (on the right hand side), past the crossing bridleway, for about ¾ mile. Past the cottages on the right, each about ¼ mile apart, there is a driveway to Westover Park Farm on the left – fingerpost Westover Down. Follow the track past the farm on the right. It curves gently right past a cottage on the right and then gently left at the approaches to a copse on the right. Look carefully on the right hand side for a stile into the copse, the same one from which you exited earlier on the walk. Enter the copse over the stile and follow a winding path through to exit over another stile into a field. Walk straight up across the field, heading a little to the left of the left hand end of the spinney in front. Continue straight forward over double stiles and fields until reaching the footbridge over the stream. Cross the bridge and walk up the field slightly right towards a stile in the wire fence. Do not cross this stile on your right but walk a few paces forward to the rail fence in front of you. Cross this fence and continue up to the fingerpost in front. This is the left hand one of two visible posts. Join the main road, cross over and turn right to return to the Sun Inn.

Brighstone

The Three Bishops

An unusual name for a pub but made clearer perhaps by a visit to the church first. Three successive incumbents had the privilege of progressing to become bishops and this was remembered by a memorial (a mural monument) in the church and the renaming of the local hostelry. Whilst in the church have a look at the unusual stained-glass windows and read about Samuel Wilberforce, a former rector. If the name seems familiar, it is his father who was known widely as being outspoken against slave trading and often visited the village. The pub is some 200 years old and was formerly the New Inn, at one time having both sign boards on view.

The landlord is intent on making his food and drink an attraction whilst maintaining a village atmosphere. Never an 'olde worlde' pub, the interior is welcoming and comfortable and two real ales from Gale's, HSB and Best, offer a good pint. The children have their own room for inclement weather, but a large garden with play equipment will allow them outside freedom on fine days. A menu of their own caters for their appetites, whilst parents can choose from the extensive pub menu which includes local sea food.

In order to cater for all, the pub is open all day every day with

Sunday restrictions, and between 5 pm and 7 pm drinkers can enjoy a 'happy hour'. Barbecues are a summer attraction. Bed and breakfast is available for those who wish to stay longer. Dogs are welcome but should not try to compete with the resident canine, who may win! Telephone: 0983 740226.

How to get there: The pub is in the middle of the village on the B3399 and can be reached from the A3055 coast road, or the B3323 from Newport. Southern Vectis bus 1B from Newport and Freshwater or 7 and 7A (summer only) from Ryde, Sandown, Shanklin and Ventnor pass along the Military Road.

Parking: Customers can leave their cars whilst walking and there is also a large car park down the lane at the side of the pub, from which the walk commences.

Length of the walk: 4¼ miles plus ½ mile extra to the Longstone.

An easy walk along the coast between chines passing the Isle of Wight Pearl Centre. Inland the route climbs through woodland under the downs with an option to visit the ancient Longstone.

The Walk

Leave the rear of the public car park by the tarmac path at the side of the green area and pass through the kissing gate into Wilberforce Road. Turn right immediately, cross the road and then turn left over the footbridge, just inside a bushy area. The path enters a playing field with children's area and keeps to the left with a hedge on the left. At the far end enter an enclosed path which soon descends steps to cross the road and go straight on along the bridleway opposite. Ahead are views of Tennyson Down, whilst across the fields to the right rises the ridge of Mottistone Down.

After one and a half fields look for a stile on the left and cross into a grass field. Continue forward towards the coast with a hedge and fence on the left. Carefully cross the Military Road and walk down the track opposite at Grange Farm. Pass the notice which indicates 'Beach and Coast path straight on' and then an 'Emergency telephone' sign.

The coastal path is reached where the path to the beach starts to descend Grange Chine. Bear right – fingerpost Brook – and then right again up steps onto the cliff path. Follow the cliff edge past the holiday camp. There are extensive views to the rear along the coast to the cliffs at Blackgang Chine and in front Tennyson and West High Downs. Continue along the cliff path to reach Chilton Chine. Chines are formed where inland water courses exit to the sea. Over many

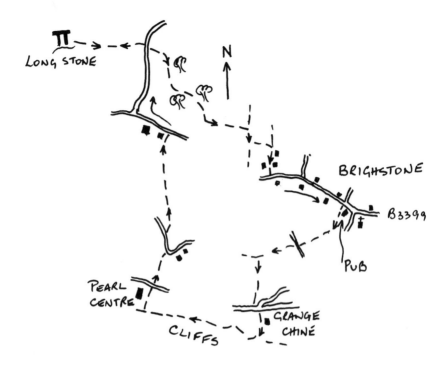

hundreds of years the streams wear away the softer rocks and soils to effect a channel in the cliffs. Some chines are very deep and extend considerable distances inland, depending on the ground and flow of the water. These chines are usually the only access points to the shore and were formerly used to launch lifeboats in these treacherous waters. At the same time they were convenient landing points for smugglers.

Approaching Chilton Chine, a large white building stands near the path. This is a former holiday centre, now the home of Isle of Wight Pearl. Entry is free, and the making of pearl products can be viewed and the history of different pearl types explained. Pearl products are also on sale.

Pass through the kissing gate into the grounds and turn right away from the cliff. Follow the edge of the grass with fence and hedge on right to exit onto the Military road. Turn left to visit the Pearl Centre, but the route crosses the road to a stile opposite. Continue forward with a wire fence on the right and at the next stile cross and enter an enclosed path with a wall on the right and a pond on the left. In a few yards exit onto a track. Turn right along this for a few yards to Chilton

Farm cottages and then go left along a tarmac lane.

Just past the next barn on the left, turn right up a grass path with a wire fence on the right and a ditch on the left. Follow this grassy lane, Pitt Place Lane, to the next road at Pitt Place. Turn left along the road for 300 yards and then right into Strawberry Lane. Go up the lane, ignoring the fingerpost to the Longstone, continuing steadily uphill until after about ½ mile a track bears right to a gate with stile – fingerpost Brighstone.

Pause a while for breath and consider the optional extra to visit the Longstone. These two giant stones are not natural to the local geology. They may be partial remains of a burial chamber or ritual markers at the end of a mound. The long barrow can be seen to one side, dated about 3000 BC onwards and is the type associated with the burial of farmers, uncommon on the island being one of only three. Legend has it that the tall stone was thrown by St Catherine from the nearby hill and the devil threw the smaller and failed to achieve the distance. He thereby lost the challenge to control the island. Mottistone, meaning stone of the speaker, suggests that this was a Saxon place of assembly, possibly where legal matters were decided.

To walk to the Longstone continue along the lane a further 100 yards and turn left up the track – National Trust sign and fingerpost 'The Longstone ¼ mile'. Follow the track and then a short grassy path to a stile. The Longstone offers a welcome seat to view Brighstone Down in the distance. Return to the main route.

Leave the lane and cross the stile by the fingerpost indicating Brighstone. Follow a grassy track curving right towards the edge of woodland. Cross the stile into Grammar's Common and follow the track which curves immediately right. Keep forward gently uphill with views of the coast on the half right. The track enters a wooded area curving left. At the end of the next short straight section turn right downhill through a more open area and at the bottom continue forward on a path. Ignore the next path to the right. The route follows the inside edge of the woodland past bramble bushes with open fields to the left. Exit through a thicket at the end and turn left into the field. Follow the edge, with the fence on the left. Cross a stile into another thicket and follow the path down steps and along a sunken path downhill. Turn right down a track and when this becomes sunken, look for a fingerpost left marked 'Moor Lane'. Turn left along the path at the side of the house. At the far end, turn right down the lane and left at the main street to return to the village.

⑦ Porchfield
The Sportsman's Rest

The Sportsman's Rest is quite small inside but has the atmosphere of a traditional village pub and is unspoilt. Very little is known about its history, except that it was originally a hunting lodge dating from about 1500. It became a pub in 1840 and was no doubt named from sporting origins – look closely at the sign and see if you can spot the animal error, the answer lies in the walk text. Dogs are still welcome provided they are well behaved. The landlord told me he has a very definite aim with his pub. It is to offer good quality at reasonable prices and he does just that both with food and drink. A tiny kitchen restricts the menu his wife can offer, but there is a reasonable choice for all, with sandwiches and ploughman's to supplement the main meals. Try the tasty fish or a steak and kidney pie. The real ale is Bass, and there are Courage keg beers. The opening hours are 11 am to 3 pm and 7 pm to 11 pm in winter with an hour earlier opening on summer evenings. Sunday has the usual restricted times.

Many walkers use the pub and the landlord says that those with their own sandwiches can eat in the garden, provided that drinks are purchased. The garden is equipped with a wendy house and slide whilst tables are outside at the front as well. There is no children's room inside but they can be accommodated if you ask.

Telephone: 0983 522044.

How to get there: Porchfield is reached from the A3054. From Yarmouth, turn left just past Shalfleet. From Newport, turn right at the end of Parkhurst Forest on the right, and take the first left and then the first right to the village. The pub is in the middle at a road junction. There is no regular bus service.

Parking: The pub's own car park is large and you may leave your car there while you walk.

Length of the walk: 5 miles.

A reasonably level walk with a section along the north coast sands. Inland grass fields lead to Parkhurst Forest, the major home of the Island's red squirrel (think back to the animal on the pub sign), and skirts the edge to return to the pub, again through fields.

The Walk
Leave the pub and turn right up the road. Walk gently uphill to the path on the left – fingerpost Thorness Bay and Gurnard. Go through the gate and along the right edge of the field with a thin woodland on the right. Continue along the right hand field edges, sloping upwards gently, with the white tower (sometimes with a flag flying) of the holiday camp in front. About halfway up, just before the barn over the hedge, turn right through a wide gap. Cross the next field with stables and yard to the left. The stile in front exits onto the holiday camp lane. Turn left, fingerposted coastal path and follow the lane. The concrete surface curves left. Just past the evergreen trees on the right turn right – fingerpost Thorness Bay and Gurnard. Cross the grassy area to the rail fence and stile footboard. In the field bear right and pass the lone tree. Walk the full length of this somewhat squelchy field to the stile at the far end. Pass through the thicket and over a footbridge to enter the caravan site. Turn immediately right down the edge to go between the row of evergreens and the hedge. Exit onto the lane by the black and white barrier. Turn left where a fingerpost gives directions through the camp. Follow the main track which curves gently left at the junction towards the shops. Pass down with the stores on the left and the clubhouse on the right to follow a wide track towards the sea. Looking left out across the Solent the view is towards the Fawley refinery chimneys. Some of the larger vessels can and do pass through this channel. At the end of the track, on the beach, continue forward along the edge above the high water mark. The path continues along the edge and it is best to pick the most suitable route at the time and take the opportunity to beachcomb on the way. There are more shells here than in the south of the Island. Go on past the green cabin with

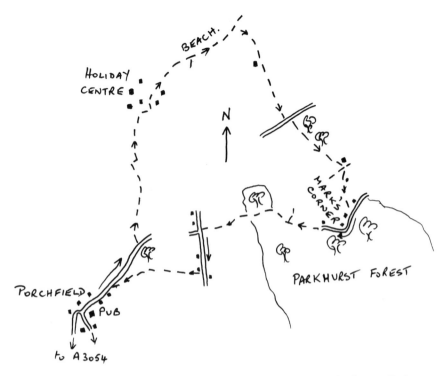

marsh areas appearing to the right. Follow the path which is off the
beach top and is close to the marsh. Head for a tall yellow marker post
in the distance. On the hillside in front, individually owned holiday
chalets adorn the slopes. Before reaching the post turn sharp right
over a concrete bridge and head away from the sea along a rough
track. Continue forward at the fingerposted public footpath to follow
the track. Go through the farm area and join the busy road. Turn left
for a few yards and cross right into the field – fingerpost Mark's
Corner. Follow the left edge with woodland on the left. Go over the
double stile and walk slightly uphill along the edge. This is pleasant
woodland of oak and beech.

At the top of the field cross the hidden stile in the corner and follow
the distinct path through the strip of woodland. Go along the left edge
of the field with a wire fence on the left. Primroses abound in the
hedge and woodland. At the top of the field a stile crosses onto the
track. This route now goes to the cabin at the top of the field in front.
To reach it turn right and pass through the metal gate. The directions
on the board are the path to follow. Now turn left back along the other
side of the wire fence and follow the field edge with hedge on the left

to reach the cabin. Wild flowers cluster in this hedge line. Pause awhile at the top and look back. The shallow valley runs back to the coast, which can just be seen on a clear day.

Cross over the rail fence to the right of the cabin into the field beyond. Go up the left edge of the field with the hedge on the left towards the buildings. Pass through the edge of the farmyard and to the left of the house, taking the track out onto the lane. Turn right along the road which is followed past all the houses. This is Mark's Corner. Look for the wooden carved squirrel on a cottage garage. The woodland to the left is Parkhurst Forest, an extensive area open to the public. The main entrance is on the opposite side of the forest on the main Newport/Yarmouth road. The forest is the home of a large population of red squirrels – the grey variety not having been introduced to the island, hence the mistake on the pub sign showing a grey squirrel. They can be observed quite often, provided quiet and stillness prevail.

Follow the lane round the sharp corner and past the converted chapel building. Continue forward at the end of the lane, fingerposted Whitehouse down the rough track. A pleasant quiet track runs downhill just inside the woodland. The track bears steadily left away from the open field in front and becomes a wide woodland path, curving through a section of the forest. Pass over a rough barrier with a stile and down a narrower winding path to cross a pole fence and footbridge at the bottom. Cross the stile into the field and go along the left edge with the thick hedge and ditch on the left. Pass under the electricity wires and continue along the edge of the next field to exit onto the road by the bungalows.

Walk left along the road and go forward at the junction towards the white houses. Just past the last cottage on the right turn right along a track, fingerposted Porchfield. At the end of the enclosed track cross a stile into the open field. Go along the left edge with the hedge on the left and the same in the next field. Reach the far end by a corner of woodland where the field narrows and cross another stile. Turn left and walk down the middle of this narrowing field to the far end. Here a stile exits onto the road. Turn left along the road to return to the pub.

8 Park Cross
The Blacksmith's Arms

Where Betty Haunt Lane leaves the B3401 sits The Blacksmith's Arms. The lane's intriguing name has many interpretations but the most romantic is the most popular. Tales of smugglers, excise men and ghosts abound and in the 18th century, 200 years after the pub was built, Betty made her name. She was a smuggler's daughter who diverted the attentions of the local excise officers, particularly when contraband was due to pass on this busy smuggling route. Misfortune befell her when she fell in love with one of the officers and betrayed her smuggling friends. Those who escaped returned and strangled her. The ghost of Betty returned to haunt the nearby fields and lane, joined by other reputed ghostly happenings in the pub itself. Enter this former hunting lodge and the traditional pub atmosphere is apparent. Several small rooms make up the public area and the cosy corners and cheerful greeting give a homely warmth to the inside. The decorations are in keeping with a smithy although there is apparently no record of a forge on the site.

The pub is a freehouse serving Flowers real ale. In addition a local brew is available during busy times, an island ale called Nipper. For the lager drinker there is a choice of stronger varieties and the driver can have Tennents LA on tap. The menu offers a full range of traditional homecooked foods. Those who have, like me, simple tastes, can opt for Cumberland sausage and mash. The more daring visitor can try shark and swordfish steaks. I am assured they are not caught locally! There is plenty of room for children in the family rooms and one of them is also a no-smoking area. In the summertime a small beer garden is available. In the winter the opening hours are 11 am to 3 pm and 7 pm to 11 pm but in summer there is no rest between 3 pm and 7 pm for the landlord. Sunday has the usual restricted hours. Dogs are welcome but need to be able to mix with the pub's resident giant. Telephone: 0983 529263.

How to get there: The pub is on the B3401 Newport to Calborne road about 1½ miles west of Carisbrooke. Southern Vectis bus nos 1C and 7A from Newport, Yarmouth, Ryde and Freshwater.

Parking: The pub car park is quite small and there is little roadside parking on this busy route. Ask the landlord for permission to leave your car whilst walking.

Length of the walk: 5½ miles.

The first few miles are flat but the walk soon heads into the downs. There are several uphill stretches with splendid views. The peace and quiet of this fairly remote part of downland is a joy for the country lover.

The Walk
Turn right out of the pub and then immediately right again down Betty Haunt Lane. Continue until a public footpath crosses the lane, then turn left along the surfaced track – fingerpost Calbourne and Five Houses. Follow the long concrete track past the cottages to reach the farm. Pass the imposing stone house on the right and go downhill on a rough track to curve left at the bottom onto the line of the former railway track. This was the Newport-Yarmouth line until about 1957. It came in from the right across the field and old bridge abutments can be seen. Follow the track on a long steady right hand curve which then becomes straight. About 100 yards along the straight a track bears left with a building in the fork. The route goes left here but first continue a few yards past and look at the building through the hedge. Please remember this is private property and respect their privacy. This is the former Watchingwell Halt, built for the use of the owners of Swainston Manor and far from any villages. The platform edge can be seen in the hedge bottom and the original Southern Region plates and fire buckets can be seen on the building.

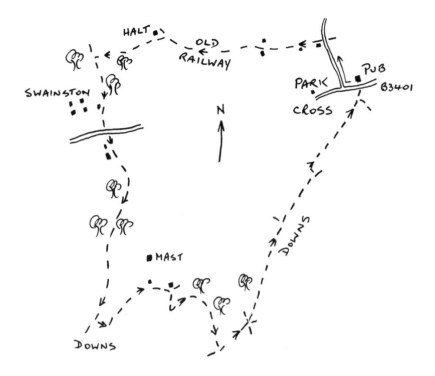

Now return and take the side track, going ahead at the next junction and continuing past the woodland on the left. The track now has woodland on both sides and the route turns left at a T junction. Go along this track to leave woodland and pass disused glasshouses. The junction from Swainston Manor joins the concrete track from the right and the manor house can be seen across the grassland to the right. Swainston was an ecclesiastical manor granted to the Winchester monastery in AD 827. The manor was huge – stretching across the island. The Bishop of Winchester built a summer palace here and its remaining walls can be seen in the present basement. Also the original front door remains with a bishop's mitre moulding on each jamb. King Edward I deprived the Bishop of the manor in 1285, doubtless an excuse to obtain Newtown with its large natural harbour.

Go along the track to the main road. Cross very carefully, almost straight over into the entrance of Ashengrove Farm – fingerpost Rowridge Down and Brighstone Down. Proceed up the track, keeping left, away from the cottages, with a beech hedge on the right. Go

38

forward up the rough track with the TV mast appearing above the trees in front. At the end of the last barn the track curves away left. Keep straight forward to the right of the electricity poles. Pass through the bridle gate with woodland on the right. The path becomes enclosed and keeps to the right, close by the woodland and then up a narrow valley. Go steadily uphill at the side of the beech woodland to reach a bridle gate and continue up the rough track in a wide open grassy area with woodland on both sides. At the top of this section bear left to continue uphill on a track just inside the woodland with open fields to the right. The track leaves the woods and becomes sunken, then emerges onto open downs.

Continue on the track with a wire fence on the left and the view forwards towards Brighstone Forest. At the fingerpost turn left towards Rowridge. However, to surmount the wire, go forward through the bridle gate and back through the metal gate. Follow the track for 200 yards to a fingerpost. The way forward is now private. Turn left – fingerpost N203 public bridleway. Walk down the grassy valley with the mast slightly to the left in front. Go through the gate ahead and across the grass to the gate into the spinney. Follow the grassy track down the inside edge of the spinney and curving slightly right. Go through the bridle gate at the bottom and in front of the white cottage on the left, turn right. Follow the track up through the buildings past the dog kennels. Just before an open field in front follow the track curving sharp left and back uphill.

Rowridge Farm can be seen below nestling in the hidden valley. Continue along the track with woodland left and a wire fence right, up onto the open down with the wire fence still on the right. This area is quiet and unspoiled and seems far from people. The path reaches a copse at the top with a new plantation on the left. The track along the top is part of the Tennyson Trail from Carisbrooke to Freshwater. Turn left – fingerpost Newport – and follow the grassy track with a beech plantation on the left. At the second gate is a multi-armed fingerpost. The route follows the arm to Carisbrooke.

Go through the gate and along the track with woodland to the left and an open field on the right. Ignore the stile and fingerpost left and enter the enclosed section of track. Go through the gate at the end and leave the track by turning left along the edge of the field, fingerposted Blacksmith's Arms. In a few yards the edge turns right at the corner. Follow this edge with a wire fence and hedge on the left. There are extensive views to the left and Parkhurst Forest can be glimpsed across the valley forward. Follow this edge closely and go through a metal gate. Before the end of these flinty fields a bridle gate angles the path left out of the field. Pass down through a spinney to reach the road opposite the Blacksmith's Arms.

⑨ Shorwell
The Crown Inn

The pub nestles in a corner of the village not far from the church and could have been a typical thatched cottage. The thatch is now hidden under tiles and the inside altered, but the attractiveness remains. It would seem to have always been a pub and the original date is somewhat obscure but old it certainly is. Up to the 1900s a village shop was incorporated and until the 1940s the pub was a parlour type without a bar. The interior now has two bar areas, the lounge being accessible for children. In winter, log fires give a warm welcome and the comprehensive menu invites at all times. The whole pub has a friendly comfortable atmosphere, and the Jacobean dresser and grandfather type chair in the lounge are particularly worthy of admiration.

The real ales, kept in a barrel rack in the bar, offer a range of guest brews – Flowers, Badger and Hard Tackle, and the choice of a meal is difficult too. The menu has a wide range, with fish pie being a popular dish, many lunchtime specials and a mouthwatering range of pizzas which can be taken away if required. The reputed elderly female ghost does not appear to diminish visitors' appetites. Outside is a pleasant beer garden with a stream whose source is a spring near

Northcourt House. The watercress beds have sadly gone, but are replaced by trees and water plants all in a shaded lawn area. At the back of the garden is a play area for children. The Crown is open from 10.30 am to 3 pm and 6 pm to 11 pm all the year, with usual Sunday restrictions.

Telephone: 0983 740293.

How to get there: The village is south west of Newport at the end of the B3323 from Carisbrooke. The B3399 from Freshwater Bay to Chale (inland route) also passes through Shorwell. The pub is in the centre on the mini roundabout. Southern Vectis bus 1B Newport to Freshwater service.

Parking: There is a small area at the immediate side of the pub but go a few yards further and turn into the extensive back car park. There is no problem about leaving cars here whilst taking the walk.

Length of the walk: 3 ½ miles.

An easy walk along the downs past areas of ancient woodland and old pits. Views across the island in all directions.

The Walk
Turn left from the pub to the mini roundabout and then right towards Chale. In a few hundred yards the cemetery appears on the left. At the end of this turn left into the open field. Follow the left edge of the field for a few yards and then bear a little to the right. Aim for a bridlegate in the hedge on the ridge in front, about halfway along. Climb sharply up to the gate, pass through and turn right along the ridge with the hedge on the right. Go ahead steadily uphill, down and up again. Views to the right are along the coast and to the left across the downs. At the end of a short hedge-enclosed section ignore the path sharp right down, but bear left along the edge of the field with a hedge on the left. Now the views in the distance ahead are across to the ridge of downs starting with St Georges at the left through Arreton, Mersley, Ashey, Brading, and Bembridge Downs to terminate at Culver Cliff, just visible white at the right hand end.

The path then joins a track. Turn left along this, fingerposted Northcourt Down, towards the mast and pass through the gate onto Chillerton Down. Turn left past the cattle traps and take the track diverging from the hedgerow – sunken and slightly uphill. Go through the next gate, leaving the National Trust area. All the disturbed ground here is connected with extensive removal of limestone from pits.

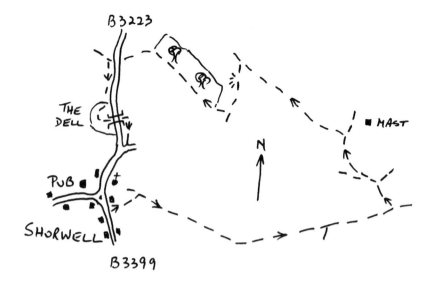

Continue forward slightly uphill on a sunken track, not the left fork, then bear right in a curve off the sunken track at the next junction, following the waymarks. Exit on top towards the mast and pass through the gate onto a concrete track, at a junction. Turn left along this for some distance and as you walk various hidden valleys unfold into view. After the straight, the track curves left and downhill and in a few yards a metal gate on the left allows access to a rough track. Turn left here (waymark) and walk along the track past the rubbish-filling and disused pit. Go through a gate to a track junction with New Barn farm below and keep right with the hedge on the right. Pass through the next metal gate and turn right past the water trough. Follow the field edge with a wire fence on the right. The copse on the right is a piece of ancient woodland, Lorden Copse. At the far end of the copse curve left keeping the fence on the right. In the valley below is the road through to Carisbrooke and Newport. Continue along the track to exit onto the road at a blind bend. Caution.

Cross the road and bear left up to a gate, not the main track in front. Turn left before the gate and pass between the wire fence and a thicket to the stile. Cross into the field. These are now permissive paths and therefore can be changed by the landowner.

Go along the edge of the field with the hedge on the left to the next stile. Cross and go steeply down (hedge still on the left) to cross the next stile into an area called the Dell. Turn right and follow the edge above the Dell. Look for a stile going right out of the area and at that point turn left down steps and cross the Dell to an information board, which gives much information about the district. The Dell is a green amphitheatre covered with ivy and wild garlic. Formerly part of ancient woodland, it was part-quarried in the 1840s. Turn right at the board and follow the edge to the rustic bridge, erected by Elizabeth Bull as an alpine bridge across the road to lead to a temple of the Sun on Mount Ararat, further ancient woodland. Cross the bridge (North Court House is seen to the right) and note the plaque on the floor at the far end. Walk up the steps, turning right along the path and then bear right to a stile into an open field. Cross the stile and walk down towards the cottages with the trees on the right. Pass through the bridle gate and down the path to the main road and go left.

A visit to the church will be very rewarding. A chapel was first on the site – built around 1100 for the tenants of North Court Manor. The present church is unusual, having three large aisles. A gun chamber, believed to be the only one now in existence, provided a defence. Other parishes had similar chambers, but practically all were external to the building and have gone. This one is contained within the church walls and thus remains. The gun, cast in 1629, now rests in a museum in Kent. The most spectacular treasure in the church is a 1440 wall painting of St Christopher. Divided into three subjects, this 11 ft by 6 ft painting has intricate detail. Also in the church is the parish record book, started in 1887 and recommenced in 1955 by the parish council.

Continue down the road to return to the pub.

⑩ Carisbrooke
The Shute Inn

Entering the pub gives the impression of walking into a private house. Not surprising, since it was built as such in the early 17th century. From 1962 it was a hotel and restaurant and only became a pub in 1981, but is still unchanged. It is however, warm and welcoming and the private house-feeling makes one feel at home. As a private house it was the home of the well known Brannon family and it is said that an aunt haunted the building. This Victorian ghost, respectably dressed, would drift along the corridors. Later residents referred to her as 'Clattie' and she was supposed to have been exorcised. However sightings have been reported in recent years.

Homemade Shute Inn pie is the speciality of the house – try it to discover its ingredients. Also on the menu are jacket potatoes, curry, chilli con carne and a variety of daily specials. In the evening the menu extends to include steaks and gammon. There are bar snacks and sandwiches for those not requiring a full meal. I am sure the cook knows you will be too full, because the only sweets are simple ice creams. Wadsworth 6X and Bass are the main real ales, with a guest ale to supplement as necessary. For the cider drinker Dry Blackthorn is available. The pub is open all the year from 11 am to 3 pm and 7 pm to 11 pm with usual Sunday restrictions. There is a large pleasant garden area. Although there are no specific amusements for children, they are welcome outside and in the separate family room. Visitors with dogs need to keep them on a lead.

This pub is an ideal base for walks and exploring Carisbrooke Castle and bed and breakfast accommodation is available.

Telephone: 0983 523393.

How to get there: From Newport, drive into Carisbrooke village and at the mini roundabout by the church turn left for Shorwell. On the outskirts turn left down the Shute – a pub sign directs. Southern Vectis bus 1B from Newport or 1C, 7A, and 7 to the village from Newport.

Parking: The large pub car park is available for customers who wish to walk.

Length of the walk: 4 miles.

The section on the downs gives pleasant views and the climb up is very gentle. The walk returns along the Lukely Brook over grassy fields and finishes with a stroll round the ramparts of the great castle.

The Walk

Turn left from the pub up to the main road. Cross over and continue up Nodgham Lane. When the lane starts to go downhill look for a track to the left going back. Turn left up the track, Down Lane – fingerpost Freshwater Bay, Brighstone. Go forward up the sunken path. This is the Tennyson Trail, a County Council route from Carisbrooke to Tennyson's Monument. The whole distance is a delightful walk but we shall only use a couple of miles.

The path continues steadily uphill and emerges into more open areas. The views left across the valley reach across to Stenbury and St Catherine's Down. The flat-topped mound to the right is an underground reservoir. Continue forward on the very distinct path. The whole route to Tennyson Down was probably a high level ancient route for packhorses or even carts from Newport, Carisbrooke and the Medina. The path emerges from a gate onto a wide track at a five-arm fingerpost. Turn left down the sunken track – fingerpost Bowcombe – following it down into the Bowcombe valley and exit through the farmyard onto the main road, where you turn right. At the end of the pavement cross the road and take the lane left – fingerpost Old Highway.

This is another old route over the downs into the next valley. Cross

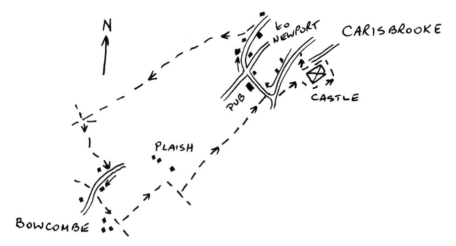

the Lukely brook and continue down the 'No Through Road' to pass Bowcombe Manor. Keep on the main track which curves left just past the manor, and go up the track with a large new stone house on the right, over a small grid drain and through a metal gate by the house. Turn left along a sunken track with a hedge on both sides. Carisbrooke church tower can be seen in front, then the castle appears, as guardian of the valley. The Lukely brook runs freely across the field to the left and the hamlet of Plaish is seen half left. At the T junction turn right up a track.

After 100 yards turn left over a stile – fingerpost Carisbrooke Castle. Go along the edge of fields with the hedge on the right. Continue over the stiles with the brook on the left. Cross a double stile. Have a look at the unusual enclosure on the stream on the left. It appears to enable sheep dipping by damming the water course with planks in the slots. The small runway would be for the sheep to scramble out. Continue across the middle of this field to exit onto the lane by using stepping stones across a side brook. Turn right up the lane. At the junction continue forward past the sharp left turn and then bear half left up a sunken path – fingerpost Carisbrooke Castle.

Go steadily uphill to pass through a gate into the car park. Walk a few yards forward across the car park and pass through a fence with a wicket gate on the right. This leads to a path on a bank above the moat. Walk along, keeping the moat and ramparts on the left. The view is right across the valley to the down above Gatcombe. At the end turn left along the second side. From this side looking half right can be seen the Priory. The multiple defence ramparts of the castle can be seen with a large main wall on the top. At the end a defensive cannon is visible. Turn left again along the third side. In a compound to the right are donkeys. These are used at the great well in the castle to turn the wheel to pull up water. Forward, beyond Carisbrooke church on the horizon, is Parkhurst Forest. Turn left again along the fourth side with the village down on the right. The mill ponds on the Lukely brook can be seen below with a fine willow tree. There were eight mills along this minor brook within a distance of some 1½ miles. The competition for water would have been fierce with each mill storing as much as possible.

Go forward to join the lane where it skirts the ramparts at traffic lights. To reach the main entrance continue past the lights into the car park. There is so much history in Carisbrooke Castle it would be foolish to attempt even a brief summary. Best is to visit and walk round the inside, with its museum and great walls. From the outside we have seen what a great place it is, with huge defences that have survived hundreds of years.

To continue the walk, turn right on the corner, down a path, fingerposted church and shops and go down the steps and over the stile. Continue sharply downhill on the well trodden path. Cross the stile at the bottom and, passing down an enclosed sunken path, exit into the lane. To visit the shops and church turn right. The route turns left along Millers' Lane with the castle high above. Walk past the cottages to the junction and turn right down Clatterford Shute. Cross the deep stream by the footbridge and continue up the Shute to return to the pub.

⓫ Chale
The Clarendon Hotel and Wightmouse Inn

It's difficult to know what to describe first about this pub. The history is fascinating, the inside is interesting, the food is all you could ever want.

It is thought that as an inn it existed only a short while prior to 1836. The early buildings were a small house known as Casey's cottage and a large building probably the taproom. This must have been the original White Mouse, which became the Clarendon in 1836, after the tragic wreck of the sailing ship *Clarendon* which occurred when she was driven ashore at Blackgang in a fierce storm. No help could be given from the shore and all 14 passengers and 11 of the crew perished. Timber from the wreck is said to be incorporated in the building and renovation although the panelling on the bar is from another wreck, the *Varvassi*. The name Wightmouse was revived 140 years later as a pun on the original. The Clarendon's greatest claim to fame is the roll call of distinguished visitors. It includes Queen Ena of Spain, Earl Mountbatten and other members of the Battenburg family, Alexander Fleming, discoverer of penicillin, Lord Beaverbrook, Uffa Fox, Edward Heath and many others.

Arguably the best known pub on the Island, and probably the one which every visitor strives to visit, in summer it's full, inside and out, although an early call achieves room, and in winter it's busy too. There is a lot of room inside with the seating mainly at long tables and on very busy days extra rooms in the hotel are used. There are several areas for children away from the bar and, in summer, the large garden with children's area will keep them amused.

To drink, the choice of real ale is Boddingtons, Marston's Pedigree, Flowers, Strong and possibly a local brew but if you are a whisky person choose from 365 whiskies – yes, one for every day of the year. Probably a unique collection. The choice of food is extensive. Starters include deep fried battered clams or fresh salmon. Those who like a 'hot' main course can have chilli in taco shells or a speciality curry. Wiener schnitzel, mussels, crab and prawn mornay and garlic are amongst the unusual main dishes, whilst fisherman's platter, lasagne, mixed grill and lemon sole offer a simpler choice. Vegetarians are catered for and hamburgers and pizzas are also included. There are snacks on the menu as well, my favourite being hot bacon sandwich. This, plus a pint and a roaring fire after a winter's walk is bliss. The pub is open every day from 11 am to 11 pm (closed on Sundays from 3 pm to 7 pm). Accommodation is available in the hotel.

Telephone: 0983 730431.

How to get there: From Newport take the A3020. Turn off at Rookley towards Niton and then bear right through Chale Green. From the south of the island take the A3055 westwards from Niton and turn right by Chale church. Southern Vectis bus no 16B from Newport, Ventnor, Shanklin, Sandown and Ryde or nos 7 and 7A (summer only).

Parking: The pub car park is very busy and the landlord would prefer walkers to use the public car park. This is a few yards further along the Chale Green road and is well marked.

Length of the walk: 3½ miles.

A steady climb to the top of St Catherine's is rewarded by extensive views. Both Hoy's Monument and the Oratory are visited before returning via Blackgang Chine.

The Walk

Turn left out of the car park and in a few yards, right up Upper House Lane. The ridge of St Catherine's Down can be seen in front. The lane turns sharp left and passes through a farmyard on concrete. Continue on the rough track and pass through the gate (waymark). Turn right uphill and take the left hand of the next gates with a waymark on a post to the left. This area can be quite muddy. Go through the gate

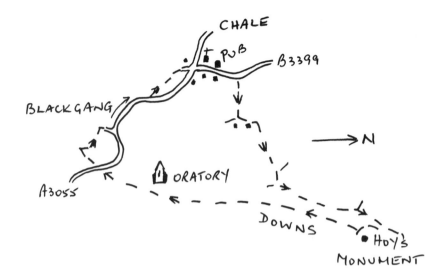

and bear left up the bank off the track. Walk up the grassy field with an electric fence on the left, going steadily uphill to pass a gorse outcrop on the right. The field narrows with wire on both sides to reach a gate with a waymark. Go through and continue on a slightly sunken track with a hedge on the right, following it as it curves left away from the hedge and across the field to reach the hedge opposite. Here there are waymarks attached to the hedge stumps. Curve sharply right into a cutting and then climb the steep bank on the left. Follow the wire fence with the wire on the left through a gorse area. A stile can be seen in front but before reaching this cross left over a rail fence set in the wire.

Views from here are along the coast to Tennyson Down in the distance. Go along the field and the route moves towards the right hand fence. The lower bracken covered slopes of the down are on the right. Follow the fence to the end of the field and turn right over a rail fence stile. With a wire fence on the right walk about 10 yards uphill and turn sharp left into a path through the bushes. Follow this winding path. There is a hedge on the left with an open field beyond and also signs of an old stone boundary wall can be seen on the left. The path continues along this hedge and fence line, passing through a shallow depression to reach a three-armed fingerpost and bears right.

Follow the well-defined route below the down with a hedge on the left. At a post with no arms (usually lying on the ground!) a sunken way bears right and back uphill. Turn right up this sunken way, but if it is muddy a footpath meanders on the bank above it to the right.

50

Climb now to pass through the bridle gate into the open area on top of the down. The route turns right here to go along the top of the ridge, but first cross left to Hoy's Monument. Erected by Michael Hoy in 1814 it commemorates the visit of Alexander, Emperor of Russia. It has recently been renovated, due mainly to efforts by Chale parishioners (with assistance from other organisations). The tablet on the other side by William Dawes honours the British men who fell at Alma, Inkerman and Sebastopol in 1857.

Now rejoin the route and walk along the grass sward. It always seems that this wide path has been mown, the grass is so short. I suspect a different soil lies here, possibly the line of an ancient track. Views left are across the valley past Whitwell to Stenbury Down and the distinctive sharp end of Gat Cliff. Go over ditch and ridge effects towards the Oratory high on the hill in front. Pass through the gate at the end of this ridge and cross the field in front bearing half left to join a wire fence. Follow the fence uphill steeply with the fence on the left and the pit area to the right. Go to the top to cross a stile into the compound containing the Oratory. This is a medieval lighthouse built by Walter de Godeton as a penance after he took part in receiving illegal goods from a shipwreck off the shore in 1314. He paid for a priest to tend the light and say mass for those lost at sea.

Cross the stile on the other side and bear half right down to the stile in the fence under the power lines. Go forward slightly left down to the stile in the next fence (waymark) and bear considerably left across the field towards a fence which protects a curved hollow. Keeping the fence on the right, follow it to the next stile. Go down the steps to the road and cross into the car park.

Rest awhile on the seats to enjoy an ice cream and the magnificent view the length of the 'Back of the Wight'. Leave the car park at the far end up steps, fingerposted public footpath and reach the cliff edge by a seat. Turn right down a flight of steps and over a stile. In front can be seen Blackgang Theme Park, situated in the chine. A visit here is interesting for children and adults alike.

Continue down with a wire fence on the right to exit into the car park down steps. Cross and turn right up the entrance road to the roundabout. Turn left along the wide grass verge of the main road, which curves right and becomes Blythe Shute. A path on the left – fingerpost Chale Church – leaves the road. Turn down the enclosed path to reach the lane to Cliff Terrace. A 10 minute diversion to the left here will show the extent of the cliff falls by Cliff Terrace, but do not pass the barriers. The route turns right to the main road. Turn left and then right by the church to return to the pub and car park. A visit to the church is interesting. Part was built in AD 1114 and the churchyard contains many graves of seafarers lost on this coast.

⑫ Shide
The Barley Mow

The railway and the main road to Newport were the reasons this pub was originally a wayside 'watering' stop. The Newport to Sandown and Ventnor line passed alongside, with Shide station and level crossing being its next door neighbour. Just down the line a siding to Lower Shide cornmill and to the chalk and ballast quarry meant a lot of railway traffic through the station. Now all has gone. The main road bypasses the pub and uses some of the railway track and a flood relief scheme now runs at the side of the pub. However it is possible to recreate the past by going into the pub and viewing its extensive collection of photographs of old times. The original pub was demolished in 1930 to make way for the present one and at the rear is a protected building which was formerly the clubhouse of the golf club and is now used as a bottle store.

Visitors who have an interest in railways can reminisce whilst walking the old track and may well meet a local in the pub who will talk about bygone railway days, but there is a warm, friendly welcome for everyone. Children have a room, and a garden area for the summer. The food is homecooked with fresh vegetables, whilst the cook is noted for steak and kidney pies and lasagne. Roast meals are available at all meal times. To complement the food this Whitbread house has guest real ales such as draught Bass. The opening times are 11 am to 3 pm and 5 pm to 11 pm, 6 pm starts on Saturday evenings and on Sunday the usual restricted times. If you wish to take your dog in you may do so.

Telephone: 0983 523318.

How to get there: Leave Newport on the Sandown road (A3020). Turn right with a tyre repair depot on the corner. The pub is 100 yards inside the turn (Medina Avenue B3401). On foot about 20 minutes from Newport bus station.

Parking: There is a car park but mention to the landlord that you would like to leave your car there while you walk. There is some roadside parking.

Length of the walk: 3¼ miles.

An easy walk with a reasonable uphill section to start. After returning to the valley a flat return includes the disused railway line, an area with water plants and leafy trees.

The Walk

Leave the pub and cross the road. Turn left over the river to the main road. Cross over and pass through the gap in the wall to reach the meeting of Burnt House Lane and St Georges Lane. Turn right up St Georges Lane. Walk steadily uphill onto the Down, ignoring a path off to the left and admiring the extensive views opening up to the right. The surface deteriorates with quarry extraction appearing over the left hedge. At the open area, with the golf clubhouse in front, stand at the gate on your right and look back. Newport can be seen and to the left of the town the top of Carisbrooke Castle shows.

Whilst regaining breath, muse on the position of the original clubhouse behind the Barley Mow. A long way for a round – of golf! Leave the open area by the track which is furthest right and walk through the gorse bushes and past the spinney. Ignore the path which crosses the track. Another track parallel on the left takes the lorries to the quarry, and eventually crosses the route. After the crossing, the golf course is on the left. Views on this side are over the Standen valley to Staplers and Downend. When the course ends a fingerpost points the path to the right. Cross the stile and go up the steps heading for a small wireless mast. Pass two lagoons on the right, then the mast on the left. Follow the track bending right and continue past the water storage tank, ignoring the track going left and back downhill. Continue forward a few yards to the edge. A waymark post shows the

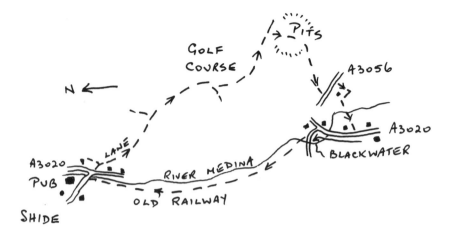

SHIDE

way down. Go over the edge and follow the electricity lines. The quarry works can be seen to the left. The path exits into an open field. Follow the right edge downhill with the tower of Whitecroft Hospital directly in front across the valley. Exit onto the main road at the bottom.

Turn left along the main road and right at the fingerpost to Blackwater. Follow the track to Stone Farm and at the telegraph pole turn right into a yard. Pass through the yard with barns on the left. Continue forward through a metal gate out onto a tarmac track and a few yards further on turn left at a waymark. Walk along the side of the grass field and under the electricity wires. Cross the old railway line through gates. Walk through the spinney, over the footbridge and down a track to exit on the road and turn right. Behind the telephone box is the old blacksmith's shop, Blackwater Forge. In use until about 1987, it is attached to the blacksmith's house. It still contains many of the forge implements and some of the equipment can be seen outside. Inside is an original brick bread oven. This is private property but a quiet look will not be frowned upon. The old chapel fronts onto the road.

Walk further along the road and turn left down the lane signposted Whitecroft. The white cottage was at the level crossing gates. Cross the stream and turn immediately right down a small path over a footbridge to join the old railway track. The trackbed to the right has long gone but once ran to the side of the cottage. Walk along the track to the left. The stream is unusual in that it has a course on both sides of the railway, probably to ensure flooding did not occur. This is a pleasant tree-lined walk with a seat towards the far end. The path exits opposite the Barley Mow.

54

⑬ Rookley
The Chequers Inn

The smart new look of the Chequers from the outside belies the age of the basic building from which the inn has risen. An early date is 1870 but quite possibly an inn was here before that time. The old inn was called a Customs House at one time, however there was only ever one Customs House on the island, at that time at Ryde. Rookley was the main distribution centre for contraband in the days when only tracks passed the village, so it is likely the excise men were billeted at the inn.

Today the pub is a bustling modern building although still retaining some of its original character. Various extensions have meant it now has a family room and a separate building for amusement machines. A large pleasant beer garden contains an extremely good selection of climbing frames, slides and play equipment to amuse the children, who are also catered for with their own menu. The adult menu contains a whole range of meals and snacks with steaks and vegetarian dishes being a speciality. The Chequers is a freehouse with real ales available. Amongst these are Nipper (an island brew), Courage Best and Directors, and John Smith's. Dogs are allowed only in the public bar. The pub is open from 11 am to 4 pm and 6 pm to 11 pm with restricted hours on Sundays.

Telephone: 0983 840314.

How to get there: Rookley is on the A3020 Newport to Shanklin road. The Chequers is on the minor road from Rookley to Niton about 1 mile outside the village. From the Shanklin direction a short cut left down Chequers Inn Road is signposted between Godshill and Rookley. Buses direct from Ryde, Shanklin, Ventnor and Newport: service 16, with 2, 2A, and 8 about a 30 minute walk.

Parking: A large car park with a field extension has ample space and your car may be left while you walk.

Length of the walk: 4½ miles.

A walk through inland fields along track, paths and lanes although the sharp climb over to Chillerton requires more effort. A quiet area with farm hamlets reflects the out of the way life of rural Wight.

The Walk
Cross the road outside and walk down the track – fingerpost Lower Rill – passing cottages, towards Rookley Farm with views towards the downs. In front of the entrance to the farm turn sharp left. The farmhouse is a well kept building with pleasant lawns and gardens. Continue along the track, then walk with the hedge on the right to reach a stream, the infant river Medina. Cross the footbridge slightly to the left, unless you wish to ford the stream. Go across the middle of the grass field to the metal gate in the further hedge line and enter an enclosed track which exits onto a tarmac lane. Turn right and a few yards uphill round a bend, bear left along another lane. Just past the buildings of Lower Rill farm, turn right up a concrete entrance track and pass through a bridle gate in front where the concrete bears right. Walk through a scrub area, then up the left edge of the open field. When the field boundary turns away left continue forward up the open field to a small green metal gate. Join the track and turn left. Follow the green track which almost immediately swings right uphill and becomes sunken. There is now a wire fence to the left and a high hedge to the right. The track then swings slightly left uphill to run along a straight flat section. At the end of the enclosed track at the entrance to an open field turn sharp right – fingerpost Chillerton. Walk uphill with a wire fence on the left to pass through a bridle gate. Continue up the short sharp climb to the top, noting an enclosure on the left with an underground reservoir. The island's water is supplemented by a mainland pipeline, the natural water being extracted from rivers or boreholes. With no open water reservoirs, the storage is in hidden underground reservoirs.
    At the top turn and look back. Stenbury Down with the Worsley

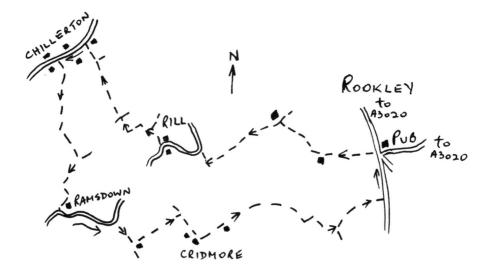

Monument can be seen across the valley and half left the Chequers Inn just shows its red roof. In the far distance left can be seen the long ridge of Arreton and Brading Downs.

Pass through the bridle gate and ignore the bridleway running left and right. Strike out straight across the open field in front but with a right bias, aiming for the right end of the line of bushes and trees. Half right in the distance can be seen the tower of Whitecroft Hospital – formerly an 'Institution'. On the other side look for a wooden fingerpost. The bridleway goes left, down behind the bushes and then sharp right. Continue downhill through the bracken with the hedge on the left to a bridle gate. The village of Chillerton can be seen below. Through the gate, walk forward a few yards then bear slightly left through a metal gate. Go down the enclosed track to exit onto the road. Turn left up the street to pass Lansdowne Gardens on the left and after a few yards the village seat allows a well earned rest.

Now look for Hollow Lane on the left – fingerpost Ramsdown. The route joins the Shepherds Trail, a County Council walking route. Walk up Hollow Lane ignoring tracks into farmyards. It becomes sunken with leafy trees growing overhead to form an arch and it climbs steadily. Note the hard stony surface and the steep rock sides with clinging exposed tree roots. This lane forms part of a through route to Ramsdown Farm and Billingham Manor along similar ancient lanes, and would appear to have been the original way across the downs. Now the motor route from Chillerton follows the valley and round the hills. The lane exits onto a grass track. Turn left and then immediately right and continue to the end. Whilst pausing to recover from the uphill walk, thought could be given to the fact that Chillerton, quite an extensive community, boasts no pub but has a village club. An inhabitant informed me that due to local influence the village had always been of a temperate nature. Latterly a village club has enabled intoxicants to be imbibed, but previously the inhabitants relied on home brews of various descriptions and many still do. He may, however, have been pulling my leg.

To continue the walk turn right at the end on a track slightly downhill and winding through Ramsdown Farm to exit onto a lane. Turn left down the lane, now the Worsley Trail. This winds downhill past quiet copses and in about ½ mile turns sharp left. Turn right towards Roslin Farm, a cul-de-sac. The first building on the left has a gravelled entrance into a stable yard. If you reach a waymark on the right of the lane on a telegraph pole you have gone a few steps too far. Pass straight through the gravelled yard to a track at the back and go along it to a metal gate into the open field. Walk along the field edge with a hedge and wire fence on the right. The view to the rear is of St Catherine's Down with Hoy's Monument. At the end of the field pass through the metal gate and bear right down the track to reach a tarmac lane at a corner.

Continue forward along the lane to Cridmore, and round a left bend to Cridmore Farm. Continue forward along a track under pine trees, then pass through a metal gate to a track between hedges. Go through the next metal gate along the track and bend slightly left into an open field. Now bear slightly right and follow a wire fence with it on the right. At the end of the wire fence pass through a metal gate and turn sharp right, noting the waymark. Walk along the edge of the field to the next gate. Pass through and continue past a water trough until the wire fence turns right. Note the waymark on the corner post. Now turn sharp left towards a bridle gate with a waymark. Cross the hidden footbridge over the Medina and follow the left hand field edge. This turns right and then left. Continue along the edge to pass through the gate by a fingerpost. Leaving the Worsley Trail, follow the enclosed path to exit onto the road at cottages. Turn left to return to the Chequers.

⑭ Niton
The Buddle Inn

Situated above the most southerly point of the island, looking down on the lighthouse, a visit to this inn takes you back to the 16th and 17th centuries. The name 'Buddle' has numerous interpretations, the most accepted being from the Old English word for a dwelling place, 'bothele'. For many years a farm, the inn's exact age is not known although a cottage was possibly there around 1500. Today's building dates from the 18th century and the inn's name appears in several sales, variously as Buddle Place and Little Buddle or Bundle. Previously unlicensed, in 1850 it was granted its first licence and in the 1880s began a series of licensees whose family connections stretched for 50 years. The stream which rises in the yard was used for watercress beds and also as the sole domestic water supply and for cooling the beer. The landlord from the early 1930s to 1961 converted the stables and personally built the models of the lighthouse and Carisbrooke Castle seen in front of the inn.

There are many stories about the Buddle and its landlords, and by reputation it was connected with smuggling. The inn stands high above a secluded rocky cove ideal for 'running the goods' and one can imagine the smugglers calling to hide the contraband or partake of refreshment on the hard climb inland. The ancient beams and rough flagstones surviving today, along with comfortable inglenooks and wintertime log fire, add atmosphere to a place steeped in history. The visitor has ample room to make himself comfortable in nooks and pew-like seats with solid wooden tables, whilst those with children can use either the family room in the main building or the converted stable block. Beware! Although welcome, children must only use the approved areas by law and the sign says 'The landlord eats children who approach the bar'. If you prefer outside, a pleasant front garden and paved yard offer extra accommodation. Dogs are allowed. The menu has a wide choice of good food, and ranges from the simple sausage to local lobster, with gammon steak, fish dishes, sandwiches and salads in between. Specials appear on the board each day and there is a varied children's menu. For those with a sweet tooth the 'afters' are delicious and fattening. For the discerning drinker the choice is wide. Boddingtons, Bass, Flowers IPA, Brakspear and Castle Eden are the real ales, with some changing as guest beers. If you fancy cider I saw Dry Blackthorn, Scrumpy Jack, Yarmouth cider and Inch's. The pub is open from 11 am to 3 pm and 6 pm to 11 pm, all day Fridays and Saturdays, and in the summer all day every day. Sundays have restricted hours.

Telephone: 0983 730243.

How to get there: The Buddle Inn is on a loop road from the main Ventnor to Niton undercliff coast road (the A3055) about ¼ mile from Niton. The turn is well signposted St Catherine's and Buddle Inn. Southern Vectis buses 7, 7A, 16, 16B, and 31 serve Niton from Ryde, Ventnor, Newport and Alum Bay.

Parking: There is a large car park and some roadside parking.

Length of the walk: 3 miles, plus an extra ¾ mile, optional.

A walk which offers magnificent coastal scenery after a short steep climb onto the cliffs. The cliff is an inland one about ¼ mile from the seashore. A visit to St Catherine's Hill allows panoramas inland. The interpretation boards at Blackgang are well worth a close perusal. Try to avoid days with a sea mist as it would be a pity to miss any of the views.

The Walk
Turn right along the road from the Buddle and then right again, straight on leads down to the lighthouse. Go slightly uphill for 200 yards and then left into a narrow lane. Walk uphill along the lane, which was the original road to Blackgang prior to the massive landslip,

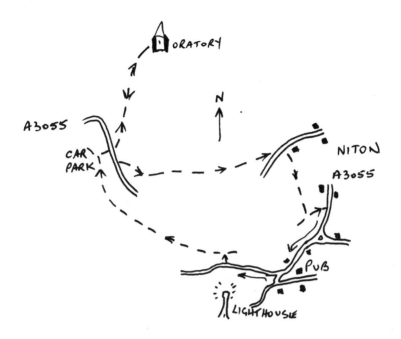

and after ¼ mile take the fingerposted path to the clifftop, right through the stone wall. The path zigzags steeply to the top of the cliff and reaches the coastal path, along which you travel to the left. Follow the cliff path for about 1 mile to a viewpoint overlooking Blackgang Theme Park. At this point the path descends steep steps but you will need to turn right along a wide and gravelly track. However, a rest on the seat thoughtfully provided would probably not come amiss.

Leaving the cliff edge on the wide path soon brings you to a car park in which you may well find an ice cream van. The car park is worthy of investigation. Along the viewing edge are seats and an inter-pretation board, and a different view to that on the cliff edge. At the back of the car park are picnic tables and a board about the old chalk pits from which the area was formed.

Leave by the only vehicle exit. If you wish to take the optional extra, cross the road and go straight up the steps. A well defined path crosses three fields and climbs to St Catherine's Hill and Oratory, known locally as the Pepperpot. Extensive inland views and the history of the Oratory are at the top, and on the end of the ridge in front can be seen Hoy's Monument, recently restored and originally erected to commemorate the visit of a Russian Tsar. From the top here you must retrace your steps down to the road and continue the walk as if you have just exited from the car park.

Turn right along the wide grass verge for about 200 yards to the first gate on the left. Enter the field and walk to the right diagonally across the corner to the stile and the end of the stone wall. Turn left up a track and almost immediately right along the edge of the field with the fence on your left. Follow the bridleway along this edge for about ½ mile and enter a double hedged grassy track to exit onto the road by the recreation field. This is the village of Niton and if you wish to visit the shops/post office/chemist turn left along the road and then right in the village centre, to return to the Buddle Inn.

However, your field route crosses the road and continues sharply up at the side of the house to the open fields – fingerpost West Cliff. The path passes uphill through a copse with views to the left of Niton nestling in the valley. After crossing the stile at the top, continue forward and slightly left to a stile in a wire fence. In the next field walk forward with the wire fence on the left, following its curve until you reach the end of the tapering field. Cross the stile to rejoin the coastal path. Turn left downhill at the side of a stone wall, the path sinking and then becoming a track. Continue straight down until the track turns sharp left and exits on the road. Turn right and after a few hundred yards downhill, keep straight on when the main road curves left. Note the unusual house in the triangle of the road. Continue downhill along the lane and turn left at the bottom to return to the Buddle Inn.

⒂ Whippingham
The Folly Inn

This pub has a long and fascinating history, and an exciting future. In the 1700s a large wooden barge was washed up on the beach here and abandoned. There were several theories as to her past but the most popular was that she was a former East Indies sea-going barge called *Folly*. The second popular idea was that she was a French barge *La Follies*. Shortly after the beaching someone moved in and sold beer and rum to mariners travelling to Newport, and to locals. The first mention of a building is in 1792 (note the bar clock) and over years it was built on and added to. A piece of the original hull timber is on display in the bar, parts of the deck and hatches exist in the roof and the hull was under the bar floor and could once be seen through hatchways. The inn was once famed for its oysters from local beds.

Today it is a large pub overlooking the river with a riverside patio, and its own pier and pontoons. The feeling inside is roomy and its timbered interior and waterside views give it a marine atmosphere.

The Folly is now part of the Whitbread Solent Inns group and (after plannned alterations) will be a Wayside Inn with a new restaurant. At present homemade food is served in the bars and the extensive menu includes local fresh fish.

Real ales are Wadsworth 6X and Strongs. Should your walking companion be canine he is welcome inside the bars. There is a family room for children's use. Opening hours are 11 am to 11 pm all year, with restricted Sunday hours. The new restaurant will be open all day on Sundays.
Telephone: 0983 297171.

How to get there: Take the A3021 towards East Cowes from the A3054 Newport to Ryde road. At Whippingham turn left (from the south) down a lane signposted to the Folly Inn. This is not the turn to the church which is 100 yards further on. The pub is at the end of the lane (about 1 mile). Beware of big 'sleeping policemen'. Buses, nos 5 and 4 from Newport, Ryde and East Cowes along main road.

Parking: Ample car park but please let the bar staff know you are leaving a car while you walk.

Length of the walk: Total 3¼ miles of which the river walk part is 1¼ miles.

An unusual two section walk full of history. The first part is easy riverside walking, and the second part is gently across fields and woods to visit a famous village church.

The Walk
The first part of this stroll is upstream alongside the Medina river, returning by the same route. Leave the inn and turn right between the boat park and the green area. A fingerpost on the entrance to the car park points the way. Walk along the well trodden path at the water's edge to pass under the trees. The mobile home park is on your left and the way emerges from the thicket to cross a footbridge. A breath of water's edge atmosphere is quite noticeable here! Continue along the riverside in grass fields with a view of Newport in the distance and a background of downs. This section of the Medina from Cowes to Newport remains navigable for quite sizeable craft and the quay at Newport still has some commercial traffic.

After a while cross a stile – fingerpost Newport. A marina is to the left and the path crosses the lock gates by a secure catwalk. The lock ensures the marina does not drain and the area is supervised by the Harbour Master in his control tower-shaped office.

Immediately in front of you is an old paddle steamer. Approach the vessel but do not attempt to board her, she is in a dangerous condition. As the *Ryde*, she began life in 1937 as one of a fleet of railway-owned paddle steamers on the Ryde to Portsmouth crossing and during the war she served as a minesweeper, returning to service

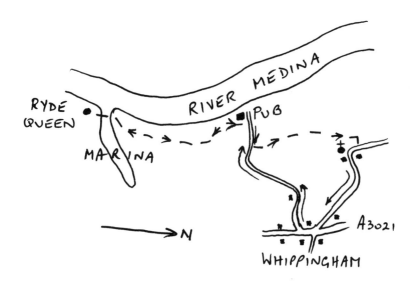

in 1945. In 1969 the advent of motor vessels saw her being superseded on the Southsea to Ryde service. Now the *Ryde Queen*, she was towed in 1972 to her present position to become a floating but static night club. Ravaged by fire in 1977, she was restored, but fell into disuse. There is talk about further restoration but presently she looks a sad sight. Imagine her in her former shining glory proudly steaming to the island, excited holidaymakers on her decks and in the plush saloons. The original paddles can be seen quite clearly and the lifeboats still hang from the davits. The sole survivor of these steamers has probably found her last resting place.

Turn and stroll around the edge of the marina. Large expensive vessels are moored with sailing yachts and behind the moorings is a modern development of riverside flats and maisonettes, each with access to the marina. This is private property so please respect the residents' privacy, but I am sure circumspect interest will not be frowned upon.

Now return by the same route to the Folly Inn and pass by the pub. In front is the entrance to the works of SARO. Saunders-Roe, now Westland Aerospace, is probably the most famous of the island's industries, with several work sites. The Folly works were in use from 1919 to 1969 manufacturing Short seaplanes and Cutty Sark wings as well as plywood and plastic products. A memorial to Sam Saunders is in Whippingham churchyard, a fitting tribute to a partnership which invented, developed and built a major contribution to the aircraft

65

industry. As well as planes, flying boats and rocket launchers (Black Knight), SARO was involved in river launches, seaplanes and hovercrafts.

Walk now to Whippingham, only a short distance. Turn right up the access lane to the Folly Inn and at the end of the straight stretch the lane turns sharp right. Here bear left down a path – fingerpost Whippingham Church. Pass through the copse and cross a stile into open fields. The unusual spire of the church can just be seen. Continue forward across the field passing close to a wooden electricity pole on the left. At the other side of the field enter another copse through a small gap, continuing across a stile and concrete footbridge. Leave the copse uphill and continue under high tension lines to reach a stile at the side of a large oak tree. Cross the stile and a small bridge and then bear slightly left across the field to reach two stiles in wire fences. As these mark the line of the underground pipe line, it is possible they will be removed when the grass has regrown.

Continue in the same direction and notice the church and white cottage away on the right. The next stile is in the corner of the field by the edge of the cemetery under a group of oak trees. The path then bears right between a wire fence and stone wall to reach the road. Turn right. On your left is a beautiful row of houses in outstanding condition and on your right, St Mildred's church. This was mentioned in Domesday although the present church is the third on this site. Designed by HRH The Prince Consort, it was built in 1860 by command of Queen Victoria. The church and its centre are open daily from 10 am to 5 pm on Monday to Friday, Easter to October 31st and are well worth a visit. The churchyard has the grave of Uffa Fox near the north wall. Famous for his sailing, he also invented a folding lifeboat to drop from rescue aircraft. Many aviators were saved by this craft which was equipped with engine, fuel and food to carry 25 people thousands of miles. His gravestone remembers this invention. The centre contains the history of the church and Royal Family, the life of Uffa Fox and Alfred, Lord Tennyson, as well as information about Saunders-Roe and Whippingham village. Refreshments at the Refectory shop will complete this visit.

The return walk continues up the lane from the church, which turns right and exits onto the main road after about ½ mile. Turn right down the road. Note the blacksmith's forge on the left, and then turn right down Folly Road, the access lane to the inn. Follow this lane to return to the Folly Inn with views across the river towards Newport.

⑯ Godshill
The Griffin

Godshill is probably the most visited island village. Tea shops and souvenir shops abound interspersed with a cider barn and a blacksmith's. It is worth a wander around, and a visit to the church on the hill is a must. Of great interest historically, it also contains a beautiful and unique wall mural of the Lily Cross. Painted in the 15th century it is the only one of its type in the British Isles.

The influence of the Appuldurcombe Estate included Godshill, and the Griffin Inn certainly has connections with noble families. Built in the 17th century by Lord Yarborough, the building could originally have been the coach house for Appuldurcombe. Certainly by 1830 it was a pub and the 1840 tithe map shows that the building has been little changed since then. The deeds list many of the island's noble families, Worsley, Oglander, Yarborough, Pelham, and a sale in 1853 offered the Griffin Hotel including stabling and coachhouse. The old stables are at the back of the car park and are listed, although the pub is not. Connections with the Worsley family gave the pub its name, the Worsley coat of arms showing two mythological creatures – the griffin and the wyvern – which appear both singly and together in many places in the area. Some confusion can arise between the

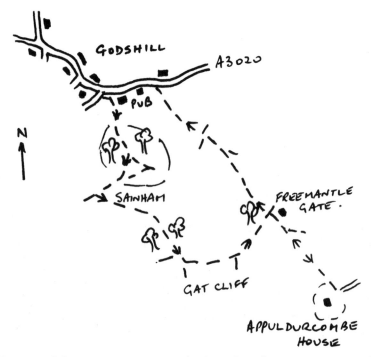

identity of the two creatures – the inn sign shows a wyvern with a shield depicting a griffin, and in stone above the pub entrance is the wyvern again.

The pub offers a friendly welcome to all visitors and is open from 10.30 am to 3.30 pm and 6 pm to 11 pm each day, with restricted Sunday hours. A good straightforward meal of homecooked food, lasagne, fish, steak and kidney pies, can be obtained within these hours, with sandwiches and ploughman's for those with a lesser appetite. The landlord offers Strong's and Flowers' on pump with a choice of draught ciders. Log fires welcome the winter visitor, but in summer an extensive natural country garden offers one a restful respite outside. Children are welcome and inside the pub a family room ensures they are in a bar-free area. If you wish you may take your dog inside. Groups of ramblers will be made welcome, and if sitting outside they can, with prior arrangement, eat sandwiches they have brought with them, along with purchased drinks of course.

Telephone: 0983 840226.

How to get there: Godshill is on the Newport to Shanklin road (the A3020) and the Griffin sits at the Shanklin end of the village. Buses 2A, 2 and 8 serve the village from Newport, Shanklin, Ventnor and Ryde.

Parking: The pub's own car park is restricted. Use the free public car park opposite.

Length of the walk: 3 ¼ miles.

A delightfully varied walk passing through woodland and a deer farm, with views from low downland and a visit to Appuldurcombe House. Some gentle uphill stretches are well rewarded by the views and easy paths.

The Walk

Leave the pub and turn left up the lane at the side. After a few yards turn left along the path at the rear of the pub garden – fingerpost Beech Copse. Follow the distinct path that runs along the right hand side of a narrow valley with a field to the left. The path winds gently with woodlands to the front. Beech and sweet chestnut trees can be seen on the woodland edges. The valley narrows still further and the path crosses a stile to enter the woodland. A few yards after the stile, the path forks. Ignore the left hand path and keep forward along a level way through bushes. Then cross a small footbridge just after a left curve. After the bridge follow the distinct route which curves slightly right, winds through the woodland and then angles gently uphill to join the bridleway near a gate. Continue forward through the bridle gate leaving the woodland and passing along between wire fences. This extensive fenced area through which the route goes is part of Sainham deer farm, a commercial undertaking for the provision of venison. Large herds of deer can normally be observed within the enclosures. Follow the path – fingerpost Sheepwash Lane – near to the buildings. A few yards past this fingerpost the path passes through a large wire gate. A three-armed fingerpost shows Gat Cliff and Stenbury Down pointing to the left up a track. Follow this track gently uphill past the wire enclosures.

Looking to the left Godshill church can be seen in its prominent position atop a hill, with distant views across the island's central fertile plain. The view fowards soon shows Gat Cliff rising sharply with the Worsley monument on top. Continuing forward on the track the view to the right opens up to St Catherine's Down with the Oratory and Hoy's monument at opposite ends of the ridge. Passing a large barn on the left the track swings gently to the right, through a wire gate and steadily uphill to enter a small wooded area. Looking back, on a clear day, it is possible to see the white cliffs of Tennyson Down near Freshwater Bay. At the far side of woodland the rocky outcrop of Gat Cliff rises steeply in front and a four-armed fingerpost can be seen. The route follows the bridleway (Wroxall and Godshill) by passing through a wire gate on the left and immediately through a wooden

69

bridle gate. Now follow the stone wall, keeping it on the right. The bridleway goes over a grassy hummock and then continues forward following the wall. Views to the left are across to the mainland, whilst in front is seen the white cliff of Culver with its hilltop monument.

In a short distance a fingerpost points right, through the wall, to the Worsley monument. This can be visited on the walk from Wroxall.

Continue forward along the bridleway with the wall on the right and through bridle gates until the route enters a wooded copse. Go downhill to the crossroads of tracks and turn right. The stone gateway in front, Freemantle Gate, is a carriageway entrance to Appuldur-combe House, former home of the Worsley family. To one side is the old gatehouse, recently modernised and now occupied, although residing here must surely constitute 'away from it all'.

Pass through the iron side gate and note the shield in the stone over the main gate. It again shows the wyvern, or griffin. The walk from here is to Appuldurcombe House and back, about 1 mile return. Continue forward with a wire fence and ditch on the right. Ignore the fingerpost pointing across the field and follow the sign to Appuldurcombe House. Pass through metal gates with stiles along the track to the House.

Appuldurcombe House is administered by English Heritage and has an entrance fee. If time allows it is worth a visit. The house is partially ruined with some rooms reroofed and being restored. The visitor can walk round the extensive gardens and the ruins can be entered. First founded in 1090 as a priory dependent on Montebourg Abbey in Normandy, the present house was begun by Sir Robert Worsley in 1701. By the time that the house passed from the family in 1855, Sir Richard Worsley had formed his celebrated museum of works of art and classical antiquities. Later the items were dispersed and over a period the house was a hotel, a school, a priory and a billet for troops. Unoccupied after 1909, a flying bomb finally removed its roof and windows.

After viewing the house return to Freemantle Gate by the same route. After the iron gate and at the crossroads of tracks continue straight on – fingerpost Godshill. Follow the bridleway forward down the track which eventually becomes tarmac-surfaced and joins the main road at a cattle grid. Here turn left and carefully cross the road to the pavement. Return along the road to the car park and pub.

17 Whitwell
The White Horse

Three stiches of land were on the 1780 lease of this pub, a measure peculiar to the Island. Formerly Chiddles Tenement, the lease passed to a brewer and in 1804 the White Horse Alehouse is recorded. It claims to be the earliest inn on the Islan 1 but it is possible that, as the building dates to the 15th century (and was not originally an inn), it is rather the oldest building used as an inn. The inn passed on to the Mew family and then to Langton's. The coming of the railways was the heyday of inns, particularly as in the early hours each day they would be packed with Irish navvies seeking refreshment before starting work. In those days, inns opened very early – about 6 am.

However, the visitor will not get a welcome here now at 6 in the morning, but come at the proper opening times, 11 am to 3 pm and 6.30 pm to 11 pm, and you will be greeted warmly. Remember Sundays have restricted times. The partly thatched building fits snugly into the village and the stone clad interior with a log fire in winter gives a pleasant welcome.

This is a Gale's pub and has HSB, Best and BBB. I found out here that HSB is Horndean Special Bitter and BBB is Butser Brew Bitter, both good pints whatever the name. All the Gale's country wines are available and a sweet draught cider is put on in summer. There is an extensive menu for all tastes, from simple gammon to fishy dishes and pints of prawns. I can recommend the inexpensive but satisfying salmon steak with boiled potatoes as a dish not often on pub menus. There is a good selection of vegetarian dishes. The children have their own menu or can have small portions from the adults' list. There are occasional specials on the board. The sweets are very tempting with the addition of old favourites such as treacle pudding.

The family room has ample space for children, and the large garden is pleasant with swings and slides for the youngsters. I noticed that quiz evenings and pétanque were being advertised as an added winter attraction. Dogs are welcome provided they behave themselves. Telephone: 0983 730375.

How to get there: Whitwell is on the road from Godshill towards Niton and Ventnor, and can be reached from the A3055 or the A3020. Southern Vectis bus no 16B from Newport, Ventnor, Sandown and Ryde.

Parking: There is a large car park but the landlord should be informed if the vehicle is left while you are walking.

Length of the walk: 4 miles.

A fairly stiff climb from the village to the downs is rewarded by the views. The return is over peaceful grassland and past an ancient manor.

The Walk
Turn right from the pub and walk up the main street. Pass the road junction on the right and the church, and look for a path to the left, starting as a track between houses and fingerposted Wroxall. Turn left down the path and have a look at the well pump, installed in 1887.

Go through the gate at the bottom and forward down an open field to cross the stream at the bottom on an unusual bridge. The structure appears to have been built to enable some form of temporary ponding to be made, using timbers in grooves. Bear half left across the next field to a stile in the corner near the old railway line. Do not cross the stile but turn right through a small gate and walk up and over the railway. This was the former branch from Merstone to Ventnor West and passed through the downs onto the undercliff edge at St Lawrence. Continue forward uphill to a four-armed fingerpost. Take the direction Nettlecombe Farm. Cross the track and bear slightly left along the open field. Join the tall hedge coming in gently from the right and follow it to the bridle gate. Continue forward with a wire

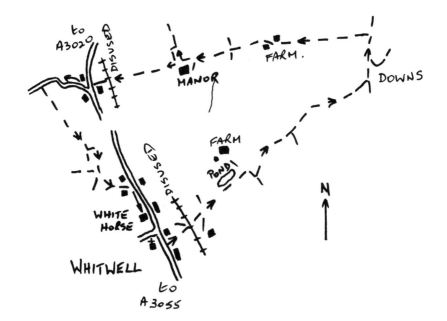

fence on the left. Note the large pond with seats, unfortunately private. Nettlecombe Farm can be seen on the left and the ridge of the downs rising ahead. At the end pass through the bridle gate by the fingerpost into an open area. Turn right up the enclosed sunken track to reach a three-armed fingerpost. Turn left – Wroxall. Go along the still enclosed sunken track with large animal digs to each side. To the left is a quiet green valley rising into the downs. After the bridle gate at the end of the enclosed part, continue forward on the track. Whitwell can be seen behind with a background of downs. The track curves slightly right with gorse bushes to the left and passes through a gate into an open field. Do not turn right along the edge of the field, but go forward past an old stile. Continue with the hedge on the left following the edge round the field.

The path now passes through a scrub area, very sharply uphill. There is a rail to assist the climb, but underfoot can be quite slippy. Pause awhile at the top for the view back across the valley and distant downs. Continue forward along the edge of the field to the stiles and then go uphill with a fence and hedge on the left to a stile which exits onto a well trodden path. Turn left – fingerpost Appuldurcombe Down. Walk along the top of the ridge and go along the tarmac lane joining uphill from the right. This is the ridge of Stenbury Down. Wroxall can just be seen in the valley to the right with St Martin's

Down behind. To the front right the view is across the central low areas towards the ridge of downs by Ashey Down.

About 250 yards along the lane turn left through the bridle gate with a blue waymark. In the open field walk forward down the left edge with a wire fence on the left. Continue down ignoring the stile in the wire with Newbarn Farm and Stenbury Manor visible in the distance. Go sharply down and through the gate into an enclosed track, which could well have been an ancient route from valley to valley crossing the down. Pass through the metal gate into the farm and continue past a cottage on the right. Go into the yard and bear half right across to a gate with a waymark, between pigsties. Turn left along the track behind the buildings. Walk ahead on an enclosed track which becomes tree-lined. Approaching Stenbury Manor the track has barns to the right. The manor house is to the left with a weeping willow in front. The present house dates from the early 17th century, but the manor was important before Domesday. The Worsley family were the owners for some 200 years.

Follow the track curving sharp right. At the end of a little copse on the left turn left over a small bridge into the field, fingerposted public footpath. Follow the left edge of the field uphill. This turns sharp left behind the copse and then right at the old barn. Continue along the field edge from the barn with signs of ancient ponds to the left. Then, just before the end of the hedge, turn sharp left down two steps to a stile. In the next field is a three-armed fingerpost. Turn right for Southford along the edge of the field with a hedge on the right. The field narrows to the end with a double stile to the next field. Continue with the hedge on the right in a narrow field. Cross the stile at the end and pass under the railway bridge, going over a stile at the side of the brook to follow the edge of the stream. Pass straight through the farmyard to reach the road. Turn left for a few yards and then right along Southford Lane. Walk along the lane past the mill, ignoring a path to the right. At the fingerpost to Whitwell turn left along the track. Pass the next fingerpost to enter an enclosed bridleway which can be muddy. A short way along turn left over a stile. Go across the strip of field to a stile and footbridge. On the other side turn right with the stream on the right. In a few yards turn right and recross the stream over another footbridge and stile. Walk forward with a riding paddock on the right. Cross the grassy area over the stiles to reach the lane and turn left along the track to exit into Bannock Road. Go left to reach Whitwell High Street. Turn right. At the first cottage on the right, look along the side to an unusually adorned archway. Continue along the main street. The white cottages on the right are Old Church House cottages built about 1574. The pub stands further along the street.

18 St Lawrence
The St Lawrence Inn

The history of the St Lawrence is mixed. In 1844 it was mentioned as a calling place for Niton carriers. The earliest part is the east end which at the low level may have been a blacksmith's. Inside, it is larger than expected and the view from the rear windows is high across to the coast. It has a cheerful interior with comfortable tables and seats. A family room at one end allows the children to enter – a vital room as the pub has no garden or outside seating. All the food at the St Lawrence Inn is homemade; the selection ranges from quiches to curries, and they are particularly proud of their cottage pie. There are also fish dishes on offer, and snacks include sandwiches and ploughman's. There is a roast on Sundays, and a full range of desserts is available to round off your meal! For the enthusiast there is Ansells Bitter as the real ale. Double spirits are offered at a reduced price. The opening times are 11 am to 3 pm and 7 pm to 11 pm in the winter with extended hours in the summer. Sundays are the usual restricted hours.

Telephone: 0983 852198.

How to get there: St Lawrence lies on the Ventnor to Niton coast road and the pub fronts the main road. Southern Vectis bus no 16 (7 and 7A summer only) from Ventnor, Shanklin, Sandown, Ryde and Newport.

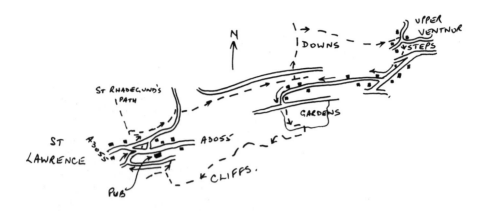

Parking: There is a large car park, but ask the landlord if you wish to leave the car whilst walking. It is also possible to park at Ventnor Botanical Gardens and be at the pub part way round the walk. In the Botanical Gardens there is also a café and small licensed area.

Length of the walk: 4¾ miles.

The sharp climb to the top of the inland cliff is rewarded by the views and a walk along the downs. The route then descends to Ventnor Botanical Gardens (well worth a look round) before returning along the coastal cliffs.

The Walk

Outside the pub turn left along the main road past Old Park Road. Be careful of the traffic and continue on the left (the safest) to a house called Fairways. Opposite on the right a path leaves the road. Walk up the steps – fingerpost Seven Sisters Road. Continue to the top of the tarmac path onto a private road and out onto the road. Continue straight across the road and up the path – fingerpost Whitwell. The path curves sharply left and at this point crosses the former railway line from Ventnor to Newport via Whitwell. The track bed now has a plantation of fir trees along it and has quite disappeared. Go forward up the path, with rails at the side. The railway line continued a little way below and then turned to burrow straight into the cliff. The tunnel is now a mushroom farm accessed from the Whitwell road. Follow the path to the top and pause a while on the second seat above the narrow gully outlet. This is St Rhadegund's Path (Whitwell church is dedicated to the saint) which gave the people of Whitwell parish access to their strip of coast. Records of 1300 show that each inland parish had a right of access to the sea.

76

The view to the left is of Ventnor with St Boniface Down behind, and to the right is Niton Undercliff. Continue the few yards to the four-armed fingerpost and turn right (Ventnor). Follow the path along the top of the inland cliff. At the end of the next field the path curves inland with the edge and follows the hedge. After about 100 yards in this direction it dives down steps on the right to a stile and then down steps to a lane.

Cross St Lawrence Shute and up the steps opposite – fingerpost Ventnor. Cross the stile and turn right. The path heads for the inland cliff and turns left along the top with wire fencing on the left. Go forward ignoring the path down to the right and then the stile to the left. The path now widens and follows the side of the Whitwell road with a hedge in between. Ventnor football ground becomes visible across the road. At a wider area with a telegraph pole and many signs the hedge becomes dense and the path goes forward to wind down through bushes. It then rises to rejoin the level of the road. Turn left back along the road. After 20 yards cross and take the path to the right – fingerpost The Downs, Wroxall, Godshill.

Follow the path through the scrub, rising steadily away from the football field. Pass old stone pillars on the right and continue steadily up under electricity wires to a path junction. Turn right, fingerpost Upper Ventnor, following the bridleway with a wire fence on the right and views over the coast. Past the stile and gate entrance to Rew Down nature reserve, which is open to all, take the main track coming down from the golf course on the left, fingerpost Steephill Down Road. This becomes a tarmac lane, and passes houses and garages to exit onto the main road on a very sharp curve. Turn right and then forward across Gills Cliff Road to the telephone box.

The route now descends St Albans steps. Halfway down, St Albans church is seen. Turn left at the road at the bottom and then right down Castle Road. Go downhill and near the bottom turn right into Castle Close, then uphill and round the bends onto the straight, where the first building, now a house, is the former Ventnor West railway station. Continue along the road for some distance, passing out of the houses through a wooded area. Ventnor cricket ground can be seen down to the left and the edge of the Botanical Gardens adjacent to it. The road name changes to Steephill Court Road and continues through a rocky outcrop. Go downhill along the road and meet the main road at the bottom. Cross directly over to the fence and find the small gate. Inside, descend steps and pass diagonally down across the children's playground and down more steps onto a tarmac drive. Turn right along the track and immediately curve left downhill, behind the buildings to the bottom and a black fingerpost. This is Ventnor Botanical Gardens.

If you wish to visit the gardens turn left here along the middle to find the café with the car park to the left behind it, built on the site of the National Hospital for Diseases of the Chest. The gardens were the 22 acre grounds, and are unique in that the climate allows subtropical specimens to survive. The hospital was a strange building, being narrow and ¼ mile long. It closed in 1964, the scourge of tuberculosis having been conquered.

To continue the walk, ignore the fingerpost pointing right and go forward on a gravel path for a few yards. At the end of a stone wall on the left, bear right up a smaller path, continuing ahead up steps. At the top bear sharp left and walk along the ridge of a sloping grassy area. Keep to the right edge with the slope to the left to pass through some bushes by a seat. Join a distinct path and turn right along it, going downhill into the meadow and forward along the right edge. Walk across the next open section heading for a green lamppost and small concrete apron where you turn left in front of the stone wall. Pass between wall and bushes to a fingerpost against a green fence and turn right. Pass the gates of Orchard Bay House and continue forward on the cliff path, not left to the shore.

The coast path continues to wind along the cliffs. Pass through a tunnel of undergrowth (or over-growth). Walk down a flight of winding steps onto a grassy section and climb sharply to reach a memorial seat. Go forward on the path enclosed with greenery. The old coastguard cottages can be seen as the path descends to a fingerpost – coastal path diversion. Turn right along the side of the gardens to join a track forward. At the junction follow the track right, leaving the diversion to continue to the left. Go forward with Woolverton Manor and clock tower to the left. At the end of the track turn left along the lane, then forward round the bends with Belvedere House on the right. At the junction turn right along the road with pollarded trees bordering. At the main road turn right to return to the pub.

⑲ Arreton
The White Lion

The original building is some 200-300 years old and was formerly thatched. It was a coaching inn on this busy road and the horses were changed here for the longer routes. Opposite the bar, in the corner, is a dole window. I am told that the poor of the village gathered outside and were handed free bread and ale through the window on a regular basis. The original brewery owners were Dashwoods of Newport and the pub successively passed through Mew Langton to Whitbread.

For those who must have chips with everything the White Lion is not suitable – they don't serve them ever! Nonetheless the food is certainly most enjoyable and filling and is served in an appetising manner. The choice of main dishes is wide and salad garnish and crusty bread or a jacket potato are the accompaniments. Homemade broth is a good winter warmer and there are daily board specials as well. In winter the Sunday roast is an attraction. For the lesser appetite there are ploughman's and farmer's lunches or sausage and crusty bread, and excellent sandwiches. A range of desserts are on offer to complete the meal. Real ales are served from the barrels at the back of the bar and are Bass and Strong Bitter. The cider drinker has

Blackthorn available, whilst those who like to try something different can have a glass of Mead.

There is a beer garden at the back with a family room in the converted stabling and space for children inside the main building as well. There is no children's menu but many of the dishes can be tailored to provide a smaller version of Mum and Dad's meal and one meal between two children can be accommodated. Dogs are welcome but need to be kept on a lead. Log fires provide a warm welcome to the visitor in winter and the pew seats are comfortable. The traditional atmosphere is maintained by the collection of brasses and copper ornaments which fill the walls and fireplaces.

The pub is open from 11 am to 3 pm and 7 pm to 11 pm all the year but the landlord does extend to all day trade when it is busy. Sunday has the usual restricted hours.

Telephone: 0983 582479.

How to get there: Arreton lies on the A3056 Newport to Sandown road. The pub is at the Newport end of the long village. Southern Vectis buses no 3 from Newport and Sandown, no 8 Shanklin, Sandown and Ryde, summer only.

Parking: There is a good size car park to the rear and side. Opposite is a large area used for parking.

Length of the walk: 3 miles.

A gentle walk on tracks to Haseley Manor (open to visitors in summer), then passing through undisturbed grassland with hidden valleys and quiet woods. A short sharp climb brings the walker over the hill into the village.

The Walk

Outside the pub turn left along the main road for 200 yards and then left into a lane past the village school – fingerpost Mersley. Continue forward along the grass track with a hedge on the left. At the end of the first field, at a fingerpost for a crosspath, continue forward with the hedge on the right. Eventually the bridleway changes back to the other side of the hedge, part way along this large field. Go forward with the hedge on the left. Views to the right are over the central plain where much market gardening is carried out. In the distance can be seen extensive glasshouses for tomato growing. Ahead the view is up the valley of the river Yar.

On reaching the end of the track at a T junction, turn right along a track and then at the next junction continue forward, ignoring the track going left. Looking left to the distant ridge, the village of

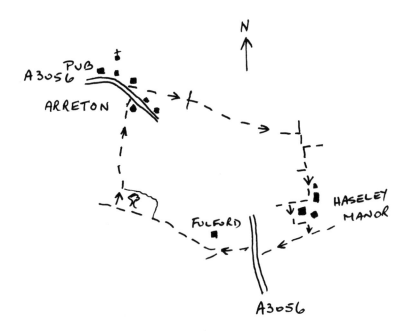

Newchurch can be seen with its distinctive white boarded tower and tiny spire.

Continue past the cottages to approach Haseley Manor and at the entrance gate turn right along a surfaced track with a stone wall on the left. Just past the car park on the left, turn left into the field – fingerpost Langbridge and Horringford. Follow the left side of the field with the Manor grounds on the left. Keep a look out for the unusual pigs that are kept there. At the end of the field turn slightly left to cross the bridge and stile and follow the left edge of the field behind the grounds. At the end of this field, cross a stile into a track and turn right down it to join the old railway line. At Haseley the monks of Quarr Abbey manufactured woollen cloth for their habits, thus introducing the process of fulling which strengthened fabrics.

The railway track is the old line from Sandown to Newport via Merstone junction. It follows the valley course of two rivers flowing to opposite sides of the island, crossing a low watershed between. Turn right along the railway at the side of the river Yar, fingerposted Horringford. At the main road turn right and carefully cross the road. Walk along for 100 yards and turn left along a track, fingerposted Merstone. Whilst walking along the track look left across the field. The buildings are the former Horringford station and the platform can still be seen.

Continue along the track curving right and at the fork bear right where a small wooden sign points to Fulford Farm. Continue, ignoring the stile to the right and a bridleway to the left. Just short of the farm the track curves right. At this point go through the small metal gate on the left, waymark on post, into the field. Walk across the field towards the gate in the far distant corner and go through the right hand gate (a red metal one), continuing forward under a large tree with a fence on the right. The next gate is a white wooden one. Pass through it and down an enclosed path to a metal hurdle gate at the bottom. Go through this and cross the stream into a grass field. Bear left up the left hand edge of the field with a ditch and hedge on the left. Continue forward with a small copse on the left to a metal gate with waymark. Go through the gate and walk forward along a grassy track with a wire fence to the left. Head in the general direction of the copse in front with a valley slope down to the right. Go through the next gate and along a slightly sunken track with a hedge on the right. A long copse now runs along the right hand side. At the end of this turn right down the side of the field, fingerposted public footpath. Walk down sharply to cross the steam and stile at the bottom. In the next field the path bears slightly left, and sharply up, to a stile in the fence at the top. Pause at the top of the slope and look back across to Shanklin Down leading to St Boniface. In the next field walk straight across on a grassy strip between crops. The view forward is across to the line of downs running left to right – Arreton, Mersley, Ashey (with the white sea mark), Brading and to the sea at Culver. The path exits on the main road at the side of the community centre. Cross carefully and turn left to return to the pub. If time permits, take the opportunity to visit the church and the manor. Both can be reached along the path starting behind the pub.

Fishbourne
20 The Fishbourne Inn

Right at the side of the car ferry complex, this pub usually passes unnoticed by the visitor speeding away off the ferry. However a visit to the tiny village is rewarding. Stroll down to the shore, sit on the green and watch the bustle of the arriving ferries. A pint in the pub is also relaxing. A pleasant roomy interior with tasteful decor is complemented by interesting pictures and a fine collection of china mugs. Rebuilt in 1935, a pub has been here since the 1700s.

The beer garden, very busy in summer, is surrounded by flower beds which have won the landlord's wife a prize in Medina's best garden competition. There is no children's play area outside, but they are allowed in the family room and also in the restaurant section. A guest brew is the real ale available – it was Tetley when I visited but does change. Strongbow is the draught cider and there is a draught mild. The wine list is extensive. The food is reasonably priced and of good quality. The standard menu has some unusual starters including kipper pâté (homemade), crab au gratin and crab cocktail. The main courses range from steaks, chops and cutlets to the fish section. There are daily board specials. Lobster is a summer speciality. For those looking for a simpler meal the snacks are good value. Salads include

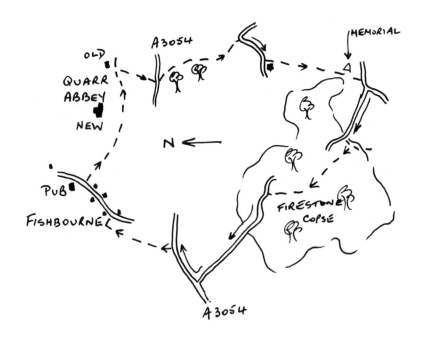

crab or prawn quiche. Ploughman's lunches are available, as are sandwiches. To round off the meal the speciality ice creams include orange/lemon sorbet in a hollowed fruit skin, casata and ice cream nests. The restaurant section can be booked although meals can be taken anywhere. The opening hours are 11 am to 3 pm and 6 pm to 11 pm all the year with the usual restricted Sunday hours. Telephone: 0983 882823.

How to get there: Turn off the Newport to Ryde road towards the Wightlink ferry terminal and carry on past the ferry entrance down the lane. Southern Vectis buses nos 1, 1A, 1B, 1C, 4, 81 from Newport, Ryde and East Cowes pass along the main road.

Parking: The pub has two car parks – before and after the building. The landlord wishes to know if you intend to leave your car and walk.

Length of the walk: 4 miles.

A visit to a new abbey and an old abbey starts the walk. Some rural fields and woodland, with occasional distant views, brings the route to Firestone Copse, an extensive area of woodland. The way back follows the road and some urban paths.

84

The Walk

Opposite the pub and car park is Quarr Lane – fingerpost Binstead. Walk up the track past the houses, through a bridle gate and continue with the new Quarr Abbey appearing on the left. This fine new brick abbey was built in the early 1900s. A group of French Benedictine monks had left France in 1901 due to political persecution and settled in Appuldurcombe House. They moved to Quarr and built this magnificent monument and after 400 years of silence the bells again rang out to call the monks to prayer. Go forward along the track downhill with a copse on the right to cross the main entrance to the new abbey and continue straight over – fingerpost Binstead and Abbey ruins – to pass under a stone arch marking the former abbey walls. Just by the cottages on the left, a track turns right and this is the route onwards.

However before continuing, walk a little way on past Old Abbey farm, which itself appears to be part of the former buildings, and look across the field to the left. Only some ruins remain of the huge complex of buildings built in 1132 by Baldwin de Redvers (constructor of Carisbrooke Castle). Closed down in 1536 by Henry VIII, the buildings were demolished and the stone sold, so that even the great Abbey church, nearly 200 ft long, completely disappeared. The original Cistercian or Benedictine monks came from Savigny and built the Abbey in stone from the quarries at Binstead (hence the name). This was the most important ecclesiastical development on the Island and the monks' influence was felt widely. They owned salt beds at Wootton Creek and had widespread pigeon lofts in surrounding manors and oyster beds at Fishbourne and Claybrook.

Now return to the junction and turn left along the grassy track, looking back to see the ruins with the Solent and mainland in the background. Pass through the metal gate and carefully cross the busy main road. Go over the stile into the field – fingerpost Newnham Lane, Binstead – and walk along the right hand side of the field with a copse on the right. Almost at the end of the field a stile takes the path to the right into the copse. Go along the trodden path, across a small stream. Ignoring any small side path, keep to the main way with a lake and open area a few yards to the left. Pass through a metal gate and continue along the inside edge of the copse, with an open field to the left. At the far end the path turns left into the field. At the field edge, with a copse in front across the field, look up to the right. Two large single trees can be seen plus a group of three smaller ones. After crossing a stream on a concrete bridge the route passes uphill between the two single trees with the corner of a copse away to the left. Continue uphill towards the distant cottages, to exit onto a lane near the speed limit signs. Turn right along the lane. When the lane curves right, continue forward towards farm buildings – fingerpost Havenstreet – on a good track. When this curves right to the farmhouse, continue forward on a concrete track past the buildings of Newnham Farm. A red metal barn is on the left and the main block of outbuildings on the right. Continue to a gate and waymark. In the next field go along the left edge with a hedge on the left and over the next stile. This field is a narrow one with a grassy strip across to the stile into the grass field. Proceed uphill towards the edge of the copse heading for the building roof just peeping over the skyline. Walk over the top of the hill passing to the right of the building and down to exit onto the road at the junction below.

Turn right down Firestone Copse road and walk to the edge of the woodland. Turn left along the path at the side of the copse – fingerpost Havenstreet – and over the stile into the woodland. Follow the path inside the copse to reach an area of dense evergreens. Turn right along the outside edge of this dense area and keep forward to cross a gully. Pass through a dense area then into a thinner stretch of beech with a red post on the left. Continue to the car park and the Forestry Commission information board. Stand facing the board and look right to see another board marked 'Forest Walks'. Turn left down the track by this with a dense area to the left. Ignore the board with coloured short walk routes on it and continuing with dense and thin areas to both sides, turn right at the next junction onto a broad track. When more paths meet go forward again and note a post marked half red and white, lettered 7/Z.

At the next junction I found a Forestry Commission diversion notice. The route can continue forward down to a stream and up to the road. However the diversion turns right and then after about 60 yards turns left down a narrow distinct path to a bridge in the bottom. This path is parallel to the usual route. Over the bridge the path continues forward and up to the road. Turn left along the road to its end at Kite Hill. This road can be busy but reasonable care will ensure a safe passage.

Turn right up the main road and on the gentle right curve look across the road by the bus stop for Ashlake Copse Lane and fingerpost – Fishbourne. Cross and walk down the tarmac lane. Go ahead on the path down and up to join a track, which becomes a lane again. Views of Wootton Creek appear through the trees on the left. Walk along the lane to a board on the right just past a house called Palm Beach on the left. The board reads 'No public right of way exists beyond this point'. Turn right, signed to Fishbourne, along the side of the fence to exit on the road. Turn left along the road past the ferry port to return to the pub.

㉑ Havenstreet
The White Hart

One of the oldest buildings in the village, the pub is at least 250 years old. Originally a hamlet, the expansion of Havenstreet came in the second half of the 19th century and produced a long straggly village. The railway and John Rylands had the greatest effect on the community. John Rylands was owner of the largest textile company in Britain and retired to the village, building Longford House. He was known as a public benefactor. The mention of this village to island residents conjures up two reactions – steam railways and the village pub – and both play an important part in local life.

The publican in 1837 served a powerful pint. At that time the Newport/Ryde coach was diverted through Havenstreet instead of Wootton. The coachman of the 'Rocket' was busy packing luggage on top, having first refreshed himself with a pint (or two). He was unable to retain his balance and fell to the ground.

Enter the pub from the front and the choice is Poachers Bar or Huntsmans Lounge. The bar is comfortable and hung with brasses. The lounge contains many interesting pictures and a collection of unusual or rare bottles of beer. The real ale pumps offer a choice of Boddingtons, Marston's Pedigree plus a guest beer. Strongbow is on tap for the cider lover and there is a choice of two wines also on tap. For the discerning diner a comprehensive wine list is available. There is a standard menu plus ever-changing board specials. The speciality of all this homemade food is pies. Steak and kidney, venison and bacon, steak and mushroom are all part of the selection. The remaining choice is extensive, from steaks and gammon through lasagne, to fish dishes and bubble and squeak. A large range of salads, plus sandwiches and ploughman's complement the hot dishes and there is also a children's menu. If there is still room left the desserts include chocolate fudge cake and honey and ginger ice cream.

The pub hours are 11 am to 3 pm and 4.30 pm to 11 pm all the year with the usual Sunday restrictions. There just isn't the space for a family room or for children, inside. However for summer visits there is a beer garden and a verandah. The pub is very popular and you are advised to book if you want table accommodation.

Telephone: 0983 883485.

How to get there: The simplest approach is by turning off the Newport to Ryde road (A3054) at Binstead. However there are cross country routes from Sandown and Shanklin. Southern Vectis buses nos 7 and 7A from Ryde and Newport, and no 8 (summer only) from Ryde, Shanklin and Sandown. Isle of Wight steam railway from Wootton (car park) or from Smallbrook Junction connects with the British Rail Ryde to Shanklin line.

Parking: The pub car park can be used by customers going for a walk but the landlord would like to know. The alternative is to visit the steam railway, in which case the walk passes the station.

Length of the walk: 5½ miles.

This slightly longer walk passes through pleasant rural fields and a lot of trees, demonstrating how wooded this part of the island is.

The Walk
Turn right from the pub and continue down the road to the steam railway station. This could be the starting point for the walk as a visit here is well worthwhile. Pass the entrance to the station car park and when the road curves right, turn half left up the track – fingerpost Downend. Follow the track past woodlands and at a junction keep right, fingerposted public bridleway. Follow the track past Combley Legge Cottage with Combley Great Wood across to the right. Leave the woodland and continue forward with the ridge of Arreton Down in front to arrive at Combley Farm, where the stream was once used

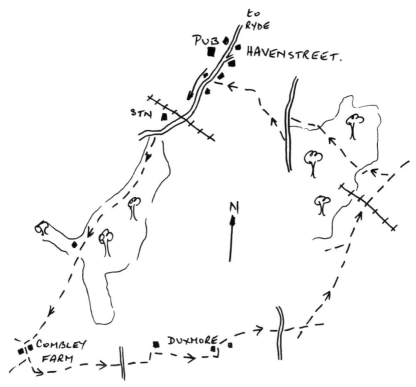

to drive a mill. The Combley Estate dates back to the 11th century and from 1609 to recent times belonged to the Fleming family. Part of the estate is now Robin Hill Country Park.

At the junction by the farm turn left to pass across the yard with the house on the right. Pass out of the yard and when the track curves right continue forward through the gate into the field. Walk up the left edge with the hedge on left, going through the gate at the top and turning left to follow the edge of the field with the hedge on the left. Ashey sea mark, a navigation aid for shipping, is visible forward on top of the Down. The view left demonstrates how wooded this part of the island is, a contrast to the downs. Continue to the end and then turn right along the edge a few yards to a gate. Go through this gate and straight across the next field to a track junction.

Continue along the track which curves left and right to pass Duxmore Farm. Keep to the right here to pick up the track away from the farm. Go through gates with a hedge on the left and wire on the right. At the end of the enclosed track, in the next field, walk along the right hand edge. Cross the high stile at the far end and continue on the track across the open field. Head for the spinney in front and follow the line of the overhead cables. At the far side go through the gateway and turn left. Pass to the right of a small outhouse and cross the stile. This is Little Duxmore. Turn right along the track to pass the house on the top of the rise, with views to the left of Havenstreet. Go along the track to the road. Turn left and immediately right through a gate – fingerpost West Ashey. Do not follow the hedge line but go straight out into the field to head for the corner of a hedge jutting out. Pass through the gate at this corner (waymarks on each post). In this field do not head for the farm, but bear left along the field, parallel to the hedge on the left. Pass the solitary oak and walk the full length of the field towards a white gate. Ashey sea mark can be seen on the right. Go through the gate and ahead with the hedge on the left. Follow the slight left curve to arrive at the end of the hedge. Continue forward to pick up a hedge line in front and pass along the left side of it.

The steam railway passes across the end of this field so beware of the trains. Cross the railway line and go over the narrow field to an opening and bridge over the stream. Proceed up the next field with the wire fence on the right and stay in it, turning left across the top. Follow the edge with trees and a wire fence on the right to cross a sleeper bridge over a ditch. Continue to the woodland and turn left along the edge to reach a stile entrance crossing right into the trees. Turn right into Rowlands Wood. Follow the defined path through, almost in a straight line. Do not bear left and cross the stream by the bridge. The path becomes wider. This woodland is very quiet.

Leave the woodland by the stile and bear half left across the field corner to walk parallel to the trees. Exit at the end onto a lane through the gate by a fingerpost. Turn left along the lane for 150 yards to the entrance to Bridge Farm – fingerpost Havenstreet. Turn right back behind the hedge over two stiles. Then in the paddock bear half left away from the hedge across to a double stile in the corner. In the next paddock keep forward diagonally across to the far bottom corner with the stabling to the right. Continue forward into the corner by the spinney to a concealed stile. Enter the spinney and follow a winding path through. Keep to the main path with a stream a little way to the right. This path eventually curves right to cross the stream on a concrete bridge. Go forward half left uphill passing to the left of a single oak and heading for a gateway in the top corner. Cross both stiles finishing in the left hand field. Keep along the left edge to cross a double stile. Continue with the hedge on your left heading for the unusual turreted building. Cross the stile into the end of the track and follow it to reach the main street of Havenstreet. Turn right for the pub or left for the railway station.

Newchurch
The Pointer

The oldest inn on the island is in a part of the countryside which is somewhat of a wilderness with regard to public houses. It is believed that an early local landowner, a temperate Lord Alverstone, placed covenants on the use of his land. Some 600 years old, the Pointer was a coaching inn on an important north/south route in one of the longest 11th century parishes of the Island. Outside now it looks an unlikely coach stop, but the hayloft above is an indication of its early days. Whilst welcoming dogs, this is not due to its name – apparently the Pointer referred to was more likely the name of an early landlord. Although a small pub the bars are not cramped and the seating is comfortable. There is a friendly atmosphere and the landlord is most welcoming. Children are not allowed inside, but there is a small chalet in the garden for inclement weather. There is a large menu of hot food, jacket potatoes to steaks, a range of toasted sandwiches, with specials on the board. On Sundays there is a roast to enjoy and the cook has a way with steak and kidney pies and trout.

As a Gale's pub, the real ales are Best and HSB and there are 21 country wines available. The Pointer is open from 11 am to 3 pm and 7 pm to 11 pm with the usual restricted Sunday hours.

Telephone: 0983 865202.

How to get there: The pub is by the church on the main street. Newchurch lies some 1½ miles north of the Sandown to Newport road (A3056) or southwards from the Brading to Newport downs road. Southern Vectis buses no 20 and 20A Newport/Sandown are infrequent. No 3 Cowes/Newport/Sandown passes along the main road to the south.

Parking: The large pub car park can be used by customers going on the walk.

Length of the walk: 2¾ miles.

An easy country stroll over quiet fields and through a pleasant woodland.

The Walk

Leave the Pointer and turn left along the main street. Take the first turn to the left into School Lane – fingerpost Palmer's Lane, Queen's Bower. Walk down School Lane past the new school and the former school house and continue along the track towards the farm. At the house turn right behind a lean-to on the right, fingerposted public footpath. Follow the right side of the field with a thin hedge on the right. The path curves slightly right and about 75 yards before the end of the field look to the left across the field. In the opposite parallel hedge is a stile with the hedge forming an arch over it. Walk directly across to the stile. The path is usually trodden across but may temporarily disappear if the land is worked or the crop starts to grow. In the next field continue forward slightly right to join the road in the bottom corner. The view to the left in this field is across to Ashey and Brading Downs, with Ashey sea mark standing clear on the top.

In Palmer's Lane turn left and climb the short sharp incline. Just over the top, as the lane starts to fall there is a track on the right to some houses. Where the track joins the lane, a stile crosses forward into the field – fingerpost Queen's Bower. The path crosses the field slightly right following the line of electricity wires. At the first wire fence I encountered a bath tub, an inefficient stile which may well have been replaced. An easier crossing is a gate further along. The next wire fence contains a reasonable stile, still under the electricity wires. Continue forward down into the bottom and pass through an open hedge consisting of hawthorn trees/bushes. The electricity wires are still above and slightly right. Now keep to the left of, but parallel to, the wires and climb the side of the valley through gorse bushes. In the field above turn right along the edge of the gorse and brambles and pass under the wires. Go along the edge with a valley to the right to reach a wire fence with stile and waymark.

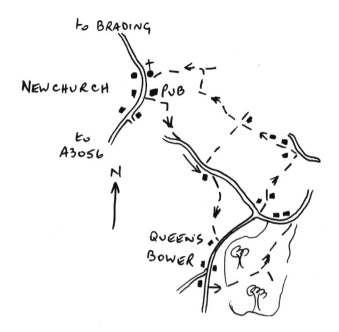

Make for the building along the right edge of the field with the hedge on the right. The electricity wires are now parallel half a field away to the left. Walk past a small toilet block on the right. You will find a camping field here in summertime. Enter the farm area. Walk between the buildings on a left curving track, straight through a yard onto the road at Queen's Bower.

Turn right along the road, and, past a junction to the right, by a seat and bus stop on the left, turn left. Pass through a small car park and a kissing gate into Borthwood Copse. The path through the copse is reasonably easy to follow but in any case it is not possible to go too far astray as the road borders two sides. Walk along the wide main path ignoring left and right turns. A slightly more open area appears and the path curves gently left. Continue with a brambly area on the right to reach a fork in the path with some gorse to the right. The right hand path heads towards a rise in the ground, but this is not the way. Take the left path along a wide path which then makes a T junction with a wide bridleway. Turn left along the bridleway, slightly downhill to an old oak. The path then rises slowly past a heavy sleeper seat on the right. Continue on a narrower slightly sunken section over the top and go gently downhill across a small open area with a side path to the left which is ignored. Walk forward on the main path with houses visible far left outside the woodland. The path rises gently and is slightly sunken and then falls slightly to exit from the copse by a small plinth and through a bridle gate. Turn left up the lane, past the houses on the right to reach a road junction. Turn sharp right along the track, fingerposted Alverstone, which curves and then becomes a narrow path near the last house. There are views to Ashey and Brading Downs. The path continues forward between hedges to exit onto a lane, which goes to the left into Alverstone Garden Village.

The route continues by turning left a few yards before the lane, along a track in front of a bungalow – fingerpost Newchurch. This immediately becomes a path with larch lap fencing. Cross the stile and continue forward along an enclosed path with wire on the left and gardens on the right. The distinctive white tower of Newchurch church can be seen in the distance.

At the end of the gardens there is a choice of two stiles. Cross the one slightly to the left and walk sharply downhill with a wire fence on the left and an open valley to the right. At the bottom cross the little bridge and pass through a kissing gate into the next field. Go uphill on the right edge of the field with the hedge on the right. Two thirds of the way up the field a stile in front takes the path to the right of a wire fence. Proceed, with the wire on the left and the hedge on the right, past the cottage to a four-arm fingerpost almost hidden near a gate across a track. Cross the track and take the path – fingerpost Newchurch. Go through a small strip of woodland. On the right can be seen an ancient threshing machine with a slated roof. Cross the stile into a grass field and follow the left edge downhill with the hedge on the left. At the bottom cross the angled stile into a sunken area and pass down through a wooded section to the boggy bottom. Bear half right and make your way across the wet area to reach a hidden stile and footbridge on the far side. Cross the stream and go up a sharp rise into the field. Follow the left edge with the hedge on the left, which then curves left to reach a fingerpost. Turn sharp right, fingerposted public footpath, to cross the field to a further fingerpost. The path can be a strip between crops. Ashey sea mark is visible again on the downs.

At the fingerpost turn left to follow the track at the right side of the field, then down the side of the churchyard with the wall on the left. When the wall becomes a reasonable height cross the stile left into the churchyard. Turn right along the edge to a look-out area at the corner and admire the view down the valley of the Yar. In the near distance can be seen Haseley Manor, with the central island downs behind. Continue round the edge to leave the churchyard and return to the pub.

94

Wroxall
The Star Inn

In 1981 the Star Inn achieved fame by being totally destroyed by fire, with the landlord and his family escaping over adjoining roofs in their night attire. Today's restored building is of the original style and layout and inside is extremely attractive and comfortable. There has been a pub on this site from about 1835 and with the building of the railway around 1865 more trade appeared from the 'navvies' who resided and drank here. Burts Brewery of Ventnor acquired the pub in 1881 and supplied beer here for over 110 years. Burts beer was well known and used untreated spring water from the chalky downs, ideal for brewing. Today it has been replaced at the Star by Nipper and Newport Best, brewed in Newport by Hartridges. Other real ales available are Bass, Tetley and Ansells although these change occasionally.

On the food side there is a varied menu, with a good range of inventive vegetarian dishes. These are unusual enough for even meat eaters to be tempted. Pies are a speciality and one unusual dish is Salmon Shantie, similar to a fish cake but with more interesting ingredients. For those with space, the choice of sweets is wide ranging with rich and intriguing offerings. Lunchtime snacks are available with

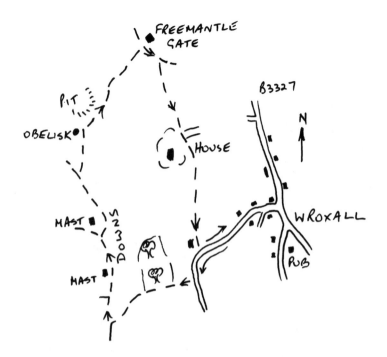

'banger roll' for those with an appetite. Children are most welcome inside; although there is no special play area outside, there is a lawn at the side and a patio at the front. The Star is open from 11 am to 3 pm and 6 pm to 11 pm, with restricted Sunday hours.

Telephone: 0983 854701.

How to get there: Wroxall is on the B3327 road between Whiteley Bank and Ventnor. Whiteley Bank is on the Newport to Shanklin A3020 road. The pub is at the Ventnor end of the village on a sharp bend. Southern Vectis buses 2A, and 16B from Newport, Ventnor, Shanklin and Ryde.

Parking: The car park entrance is in the lane at the side of the pub and is not large. You may leave the car while you walk but the landlord would like to know.

Length of the walk: 3¾ miles.

A walk along the ridge with a steady climb up and spectacular views. After a steep descent, the return is through parkland and grassy fields.

96

The Walk

Leave the pub and turn left, downhill on the main road to the corner shop. Turn left along West Street through the houses and continue along the narrow lane beyond. The lane turns sharp left and then, after about 100 yards, take the right turn up another surfaced lane. Follow this uphill onto Stenbury Down with views to the left, of Upper Ventnor. Through the shallow gap in the downs, the sea can be glimpsed in the distance. At the top the lane curves right along the top of the ridge towards wireless masts. Pass one wireless station and continue to the end of the lane at the gateway to station number two. Take the path to the right along the high wire fence-line – fingerpost Gat Cliff and Sainham. The route passes down between fence and stone wall cum.scrub hedge. Views from here across the valley show Brading Down in the distance with the Sandown/Shanklin area to the right. Culver Cliff is in the background.

Keep to the path by the fence to the first stile. You may see deer in the enclosures as this is a commercial deer farm. Turn right over the stile – fingerpost Worsley Monument. Cross the field heading towards the monument, over another stile and on to reach the obelisk, which was erected in 1774 by Sir Richard Worsley of Appuldurcombe, in memory of Sir Robert Worsley who died in 1747. It was severely damaged in 1831 after a lightning strike but was restored in 1983 by another Sir Richard Worsley with help from the Isle of Wight County Council and the people of Godshill parish. Stand in front of the plaque and the view is of Stenbury Down with the sea visible half left through the shallow gap over Upper Ventnor. Sharp left Wroxall village can be seen.

To the right Niton village can be seen nestling in a gap in the downs and to the extreme right is St Catherine's Down with the Oratory and Hoy's Monument at opposite ends of the ridge. Now stand on the other side of the monument and the view is across the Solent to the mainland. In the immediate foreground is Godshill with its hilltop church, whilst to the left the view is down the island towards Yarmouth. In the extreme left can be seen the distant white cliff of Tennyson Down. Looking to the right one can see Sandown and Shanklin with Culver Cliff in the background.

Leave the monument by walking away in the direction of Wroxall village below. Curve steadily left along the top edge of a sharp drop to an old quarry, walking steadily downhill. Pass close to a wire fence on your right. When the fence turns to run away from the route continue forward and downhill. Then bear slightly left, sharply down a slight path to head for the stone wall across the bottom. Look for a stone stile in the wall and a fingerpost. Cross the wall and turn right to follow the wall along the bridleway. Go through bridlegates and into a small copse. Walk downhill to the crossroads of tracks and turn right. Pass through the side gate of Freemantle Gate. The stone gateway is the carriageway entrance to Appuldurcombe House. To one side is the old gatehouse, recently modernised and now occupied. Note the shield above the gate with a wyvern/griffin figure. Continue forward with the wire fence and ditch on the right. Ignore the fingerpost pointing across the field, and follow the sign to Appuldurcombe House. The path crosses metal gates with stiles and passes down the track to the House. For information about the House please refer to the walk from Godshill.

Facing the entrance to Appuldurcombe House turn left down the track a few yards and then immediately right over a stile to follow a path along the edge of the field. The stone wall is on the right along the field. Partway along the wall, view the house across the lawn, and note the small arched side gate through the wall. Ignore the fingerpost pointing left across the field and continue along the estate boundary. Where this turns sharp right, cross the stile and continue forward along the track – fingerpost Span. Pass Span Lodge on the right and rejoin the lane at the sharp bend. Turn left along the lane to return to Wroxall and the pub.

24 Ventnor
The Spyglass Inn

The town has many historic connections and the walk will show some of them, but pause awhile first at the Spyglass and absorb the atmosphere and conviviality of a seafaring pub. It was built about 1830 as a bath house and the salt water used would have assisted in the healthiness of the residents and visitors who came to 'take the air and the waters'. The oldest building on the esplanade, it has had a chequered life. In the 1890s a signal station, marked on maps, was possibly sited on or near the building, and in later years it has been both flats and a hotel, with fire destroying some of it. Five years ago it was turned into a pub and began to gain the reputation it has today.

The extensive menu caters for all tastes, with reasonably priced dishes offering good value. Sandwiches, ploughman's and jacket potatoes supplement the main menu whilst children have their own selection. The dishes are homemade with many daily specials on the board. When available, local crab and lobster are served and the Spyglass seafood platter is well known. This pub is open all day May to September, with winter hours of 10.30 am to 3 pm and 7 pm to 11 pm, and the usual Sunday restrictions. This is a freehouse with real ales of Burton, a guest ale and Spyglass Kingrock Ale and a good range of cider, bottled drinks and spirits complete the bar. The many rooms are a treat to investigate. There is a family room but children can be accommodated elsewhere if demand necessitates. The interior reflects the landlord's interest in antiques. Seafaring items of all description adorn each room – and they are genuine articles. Posters, pictures, binnacles, floats, pots – all add to the enjoyment of a visit here. During the warm sunny weather enjoyed in Ventnor there is a covered patio and an open paved area overlooking the sea. Sheltered from the wind and facing the sun, it is amazing how often sitting out is possible.

The landlord welcomes walkers – and well behaved dogs! He can also offer bed and breakfast accommodation. Call in at any time and enjoy a meal, but on certain days there are special events. A Beaujolais breakfast has been known, and every year the Smugglers Pageant on the esplanade and beach brings a touch of times past to Ventnor and the Spyglass. Live music, too, is featured from time to time.

Telephone: 0983 855338.

How to get there: Head through the town for the sea front and the pub is at the western end of the esplanade. Southern Vectis buses nos 2A, 16, 16B, 7 and 7A from Newport, Shanklin, Sandown, and Ryde (Freshwater in summer only).

Parking: The pub car park is very small. There is some roadside parking on the front, but best of all continue up the slope behind the inn to the large public car park (parking charge).

Length of the walk: 3 ¼ miles.

This short walk has probably the most strenuous climb on the island. From sea level to the top of St Boniface is 787 ft in height and the view is marvellous. Some of the walk is through the town's streets with interesting buildings and some on the open downs.

The Walk
Stroll along the esplanade from the pub and have a look in the longshoreman's shop at the many seafaring items. Opposite the arcade, on the edge of the sea wall, look for a tall iron pedestal with a ball and point on top. At noon the shadow falls across a row of stones in the pavement and over to a plaque in the entrance floorway of the arcade. The plaque indicates the position in degrees and minutes. Further along is the Victorian clock and weather station. When the road leaves the front, walk up the slope off the promenade. The Cascade gardens appear below, a pleasant water garden formed where a natural stream which never dries up flows out. The massive

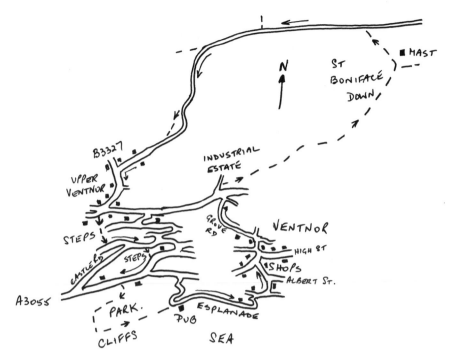

arches the slope is built on have a military look from below so this area is called the Battery. Pass the Winter Gardens at the top of the winding slope to a junction to the right of Alexander Gardens. Pier Street continues forward and was originally Mill Street up to about 1880. On this corner stood a small corn grist mill with the mill pond and water-meadows behind. The first reference to a mill on this site was 13th century.

The route continues into the town along Pier Street to the traffic lights. Bear right here and then cross the road. Note the Country House Tearooms – an ornate building probably typical of Victorian times. Pass to the left side of the building, steeply up a lane called Tulse Hill. Continue to the end past interesting small cottages clinging to the slope. At the end turn left and uphill again in Grove Road.

Continue forward uphill as Grove Road gets steeper. Exit onto the main road at the top opposite the Terminus Hotel. The building and clock tower to the right are typical Victorian utility buildings of the Ventnor Gas & Water Company, built in 1883. Some of Ventnor's water still comes from the natural springs in the old railway tunnel. The town was the first on the island to be lit by electricity in 1899.

Cross the road and pass round the hotel into the trading estate, established on the site of the railway station. The caves in the steep cliffs were used for storage and workshops and are even now occupied by small businesses.

The path out to the Down starts behind the Terminus Hotel – fingerpost Coastal Path Luccombe. Go up steps and along the enclosed path to the National Trust area of St Boniface Down. Cross the stile and up more steps. Climb steeply up, ignoring a stile to the right. Part way up, a pause must be taken to gain some breath! Look back for the view across Ventnor and the coast and consider how far the climb has been so far from sea level. Continue up, generally following the line of the fence on the right. The path then bears sharply left from the fence to the top of a hump of ground. At the top walk along the top of the ridge towards an aerial mast with a building at the base. Eventually a fence runs along the right of the path which continues forward to the enclosure at the base of the aerial mast.

Do not pass through the gate but follow the fingerpost (Wroxall and Ventnor) and walk along the left side of the enclosure fence. It is a narrow path with the fence on the right. The view here to the left is of St Catherine's Down with the Oratory and the white cliff top of Tennyson Down. At the end cross a stile into a small car park area with a stone plinth and information board. This is the highest point on the island at 787 ft above sea level. This side of the Down has been invaded by holm or evergreen oak which spread from the gardens of Ventnor in the last century. It was originally kept in check by the donkeys which grazed here. Reduced grazing allowed colonisation to the detriment of natural flowers, so wild goats have been brought in to restore the balance. The radar station belongs to the Civil Aviation Authority, part of a chain monitoring all aircraft movements. It seems that prehistoric man was an early farmer on this site. Ancient pollens in the burial mounds survived in the acid soil and show that grass and cereals were grown.

Cross the car park to the lane and turn left along it. Views across the island to the right show the Solent and the chimneys of Fawley oil refinery. Go forward ignoring two fingerposts right to Wroxall. The lane then starts to zigzag down with a gate on the right, fingerposted Upper Ventnor. Go through the gate, bear left downhill and at the crossroads of paths continue forward, fingerposted bridleway, downhill to rejoin the lane. At the end of the lane turn left (right for an ice cream) and cross over the main road. Pass the public conveniences and continue round the bend to reach the fish and chip shop on the corner. Cross Gills Cliff Road towards the telephone box opposite and descend St Albans Steps at the side. Go all the way down the steps, a very long flight but not so bad in this direction. At the bottom turn left along the road, past the first junction on the right and round the bends. Cross over to two benches on the right and just past the junction of Castle Road and Zig Zag Road look for more steps. These are at the end of the wall on the right where the pavement ends. Descend again.

At the bottom turn right and follow the road round the bends towards Ventnor Park. Cross over and walk along to the park buildings. Turn left through the double gates and then forward along the path in front which curves gently right. There is a tea kiosk to the left. Continue along the broad path past the toilets and bandstand to the far end of the park. A stream flows to one side and flower beds make a pretty setting to a peaceful green strip. At the end follow the path curving left uphill and over the top. A grassy sward is to the left and a children's play area to the right. Go straight over through an exit towards the sea and down the left hand steps. Bear left along the path, shelving down. Another tarmac path rises from the right to join. Continue forward over a hump to descend right to the cliff top. Return on the cliff top path to the car park above the Spyglass. The large piece of stone set in concrete is part of a huge quantity brought from Scotland to form the sea defences below.

Descend to sea level again. The height change on the walk has been 1574 ft, nearly ⅓ mile and the average slope has been similar to walking up and down a 1 in 10 hill all the way.

㉕ **Bonchurch**
The Bonchurch Inn

Walking down Bonchurch Shute the sign at the entrance drive to the pub gives no indication of the hidden delights behind the rocky walls. Bonchurch Inn is the place to try Italian specialities, under the guidance of the licensee, Ulisso Besozzi. Offering a range of both English and Italian dishes, the menu satisfies most tastes. Sandwiches and snacks are also available. Real ales on offer are Flowers Original and Boddingtons – to be sampled in an atmosphere little changed from the early 1800s. In summer there is a courtyard to sit in, whilst a family room caters for the children. There is also some bed and breakfast accommodation.

The Bonchurch Inn buildings around the yard were originally the stables and coach house of the hotel built in 1840, which was behind the coach house. Across the yard from the inn, formerly stables, is the stone building which was the first inn – taproom at the front and living accommodation at the rear. Sit in front of the inn with a pint and muse on the early activities in the yard. Bustling with coaches, horses and people this was an important terminus. In 1881 coaches left for the station and through to Freshwater with a return in the afternoon and regular services to the station and Ventnor. The hotel thrived with American and German visitors.

Times have changed and now refreshment can only be obtained between 11 am to 2.30 pm, 6.30 pm to 11 pm, with restricted hours on Sunday.

Telephone: 0983 852611.

How to get there: From Shanklin take the A3055 towards Ventnor. Turn left down Bonchurch Shute shortly after the Smugglers Haven. From Ventnor town head for Shanklin and taking a right turn by the Holy Trinity church, signposted Bonchurch, pass through the village and out up Bonchurch Shute. Southern Vectis buses 16, 7 and 7A pass Upper Bonchurch, 16B and 2A go to Ventnor Town (1½ miles).

Parking: There is really no pub car park, but careful parking in Bonchurch Shute is no problem.

Length of the walk: 4½ miles.

A very strenuous start to the walk climbing to the top of the downs. Thereafter an easy section down to Shanklin with a return along the coast through the interesting landslip. Arguably the best walk in the area for variety.

The Walk

From the inn turn right downhill and by the post box bear right into 'The Pitts', a cul-de-sac. A little way along the lane, at Greycliff Luxury Apartments, turn right. A fingerpost on the left points right to Upper Bonchurch and Leeson Road. Pass across the parking area and up the steps at the back. Climb the stone steps up the cliff to the road with views across Bonchurch to the coast. At the top turn left along the road and cross over. Turn right up a path with steps and fingerpost – Wroxall and Shanklin. Go through a gate onto the downs and bear slightly right up wooden steps. Continue forward, passing to the left of a small group of bushes and cross over a left/right path. Continue steeply up to pass to the right of the densest part of the bushes in front, heading for the highest and steepest slope. Pass through the bushy area and the gate at the top to reach the wooden fingerpost. The wired enclosure contains a small herd of wild goats to control the growth of the scrub, holm oak.

This steep climb will necessitate many pauses, and views across Ventnor and the coast can be enjoyed. Bear slightly right at the fingerpost to pass in front of the car park with the barriers on the left, to reach an information board on a stone plinth.

Continue with barriers on the left. Walk forward to reach a limestone track running onto the ridge in front. The barriers round the car

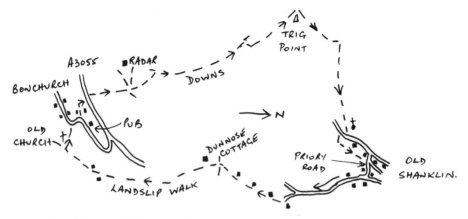

park will curve left away from the path. Keep on the track to cross signs of a ditch and pass a mound on the left. The path curves slightly left and makes a T junction with another main track. At this point the view is into a valley with Wroxall in the distance in the bottom. Turn right along the ridge with the valley to the left. Continue to a gate plus bridlegate. Go through and turn sharp right, fingerposted Luccombe, and after a few yards on the grass, sharp left into a grassy track between hedges, fingerposted Shanklin.

Cross the stile into the field and follow the left hand side with the fence and bushes on the left. Views to the right are across Luccombe and Shanklin to Sandown and Culver Cliff beyond. Ignore the group of fingerposts on the left and continue forward, aiming for the white trig point on top of the hill in front. Turn right at the point and head for Shanklin below (blocks of white buildings). The route over the grass shows a slight depression and a crater can be seen just to the right. Continue down, heading for a gate in the corner of the far side of the field. Cross the stile by the gate and walk down the edge of the field between wire and hedge. At the fingerpost at the bottom turn right. Continue along the edge of these fields, crossing stiles. The path curves left downhill and down steps to a stile. Cross the next field, which is a strip, to a post opposite, then go steeply down slippy steps through gorse and forward to the next stile. Across the next fields the path is usually well defined and heads for the spire of St Blasius' church in the woodland in front. Cross the stile into the grass field and head across towards a section of fence into the woodland. Pass through the trees, across the churchyard and through the lychgate (note the inscription).

Turn right and carefully cross to the other side of the road. Cross the bridge and turn left down a track, passing down through the school to exit into Priory Road. Turn right uphill and at the end turn right – fingerpost Coastal Path and Luccombe Tea Gardens. Follow the road uphill and at the end of the hotels on the right it is possible to cross into the field to avoid walking along the road – fingerpost Coastal Path. The lane is rejoined further along after walking along inside the hedge.

Note the ancient gas lamps, still in use. Go along the lane and over at the junction – fingerpost Luccombe Tea Gardens. The right turn goes into Luccombe garden village. At the end of the lane bear right along a path – fingerpost Coastal Path Luccombe. This passes through a landslip area and parts of the village have collapsed. This land slippage has been caused by draining water gathering in the blue slipper clay under the rock layers. Pressure from above causes the ground to slide over the clay. At the sea the cliff slips and is washed away thus allowing further falls. Luccombe fishing village has disappeared due to the receding cliffs. In the garden village the movement has caused ground sinkage over large areas – still continuing to some extent today.

Follow the path through this area and go forward at the next junction – fingerpost Luccombe Chine and Ventnor. The route passes through Luccombe tea gardens and on to thatched Dunnose Cottage which serves refreshments, and has a pleasant flower garden and a large aviary. Continue forward along the track past the cottage to enter the Bonchurch landslip area at an information board. Ignore the path to the right.

Continue forward to the iron gates and bear right into an enclosed path. Note the apt ditty on the board. Follow the path by the wall and down steps, then winding through the undercliff. In a while the wishing seat is passed, a piece of fallen rock forming a seat shape. At the path junction go straight on – fingerpost Bonchurch and Ventnor.

This next section has had extensive work on boardwalks and steps. Follow the clear main path to the far end of the landslip (another information board) and go down the path to the cottages. Continue to the Boathouse Cottage on the left. Just past this turn right through a stone wall and cross the grass on top of the slope with a wire fence on the right. This is Monks Bay. At the end of the grass bear right with the fence to exit into a lane. Walk up the lane – but visit the church first.

Continue uphill right and left past East Dene on the right. This building, now a schools' centre, was formerly the home of the romantic poet Swinburne, now buried in Bonchurch New Church. At the next junction turn right up Bonchurch Shute to return to the inn.

26 Brading
The Bugle Inn

In coaching times the Bugle was one of the most important inns on the Island for the exchange of horses and was also a post house for the collection and delivery of mail. The original Brading quay was close by the bottom of the car park and a tiny attic window at the rear overlooks the former Haven and was used as a smugglers' look-out to give warning of revenue officers. Legend has it that King Charles I took refuge here in a secret cupboard to avoid Cromwell's men.

Although a very old building (1314), its position on a busy road does not enhance its looks, but inside the landlord and his staff offer a warm welcome and live up to the awards they have won. 'Innkeper of the year' several times, 'family pub of the year', 'best pub loos', plus many other certificates, set the scene. The interior is large and traditional and the food and drink outstanding.

Open in winter from 10.30 am to 3 pm and 6 pm to 11 pm and in summer all day 11 am to 11 pm with Sunday having the usual restricted times, the Bugle offers a range of facilities. Real ales on pump are Flowers Original, Marston's Pedigree and Boddingtons, with a guest ale changing regularly. If you are keen on cider, Scrumpy Jack and Strongbow are on tap plus many bottled varieties. To complement and complete the food there is a choice of 13 vintage ports, 6 brandies, 56 liqueurs and a wide selection of wines by the glass and bottle. With such a large selection of drinks, customers may look for a large selection of meals and they will not be disappointed. The menu ranges from steaks to sandwiches plus daily specials, four in winter and eight in summer. Sunday roasts are a speciality and the visitor can even choose the size, large, medium and child's, all excellent value. The steak and kidney pie is renowned and all the meals are home cooked and served with fresh vegetables. Two rooms provide an à la carte restaurant which should be booked in advance.

Dogs must wait outside, perhaps in the beer garden, as all areas are for dining, but children are well looked after inside where they have a choice of indoor games and toys, and playpens and high chairs are available. The tots are considered even in the loos where the baby changing facilities are excellent – even the gents is equipped so that dad can take his turn. The landlord and his staff are only too willing to be helpful and visitors should leave being well satisfied.

Telephone: 0983 407359.

How to get there: The inn is situated in the middle of Brading on the main through road (A3055). Southern Vectis buses nos 16, 16B, 7 and 7A, from Sandown, Ventnor, Shanklin and Ryde. Trains from Shanklin, Sandown and Ryde.

Parking: The large pub car park can be used. Please let bar staff know if you leave your car there while you walk.

Length of the walk: 3 miles.

A pleasant walk below the down, passing Nunwell House, with a stroll around historic Brading at the end.

The Walk
Turn left out of the pub car park along the road. When it turns left, go over the zebra crossing. Turn left up the side street (Mall Road) and go uphill, curving left and right and then right up a track – fingerpost Nunwell. The sunken bridleway climbs steadily with views to the right back over the town. The way passes an old chalk pit on the left and continues uphill on the main path, another main path trailing in from the left. Continue forward over the crest and now slightly downhill, remaining on the main route and ignoring the side path with a fingerpost to Nunwell.

The path now becomes a wider track. Note an avenue of lime trees on the right running towards Nunwell House. Continue forwards

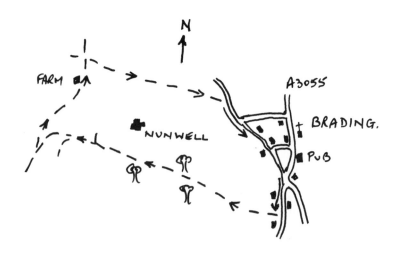

slightly uphill with three yew trees at the side. A fingerpost appears on the left, in a small open area, and points right to a bridleway to Ryde. Continue forward in the direction of Newchurch. The view to the right is of Ryde in the distance with its distinctive church spire on the skyline. Across the Solent, Portsmouth can be seen.

Pass through a metal gate and continue forward. Note the fingerless fingerpost in a few yards with a track bearing left. Ignore this turn and keep on with the hedgeline on the right for about 25 yards. Now follow a green trackway curving left gently and leaving the hedgeline. Keep along this track as it heads into a rising valley. Observe another rough track coming up the valley bottom to meet this one and turn right downhill to join it, going back down it with a wire fence on the left.

Pass through a gate, heading for farm buildings in front. At the barns, bear right round them, through the slurry pit area and turn left down the main track. Go down the tarmac farm lane to the point where a public footpath crosses the lane. Turn right over a stile – fingerpost Brading. Walk directly across the field bearing slightly right. Over the brow of the rise the stile is in the fence line in front, just to the left of a large oak tree. Cross the stile and footbridge. Continue forward just slightly left to a tree with a waymark fastened to it, on the brow of the rise. Follow the direction of the arrow to pass under electricity wires midway between two pylons. In the distance ahead is a fingerpost.

Nunwell House lies to the right in the trees. The Oglander family, from Normandy, was established here about 1100 and lived in the house continuously for over 850 years – an incredible period. The history of this family is fascinating and their descendants had much to do with the early foundations on the island. The house is open to the public during the summer season and a visit will explain much about the development of the island and its manor houses.

From the fingerpost continue forward with the hedge on the left for a short distance and then across to the hedgeline in front with yet another fingerpost. Cross the open field to a gathering of oaks. Pass through the trees and on to the next hedgeline where the path exits onto the road. Turn right, past the entrance to Nunwell House and then bear right along a narrow lane. Do not go up the fieldpath sharp right but continue along the lane and where the lane forks, with houses all round, take the left fork. This exits into the main street of Brading. Turn right to return to the pub or take the opportunity to investigate historic Brading.

Inside the church, one of the Island's oldest, are tombs to commemorate many of the Oglander family, and indeed there is an Oglander chapel, a most attractive feature. There is also a tomb to 'Little' Jane Squibb who died in 1799. She appeared in possibly the world's first bestseller, a book entitled *Annals of the Poor*, written by the then curate in charge. The church has unusual stairs to the tower and spire. Close by on the corner of Quay Lane, is the village gaol and stocks with the Town Hall above. In the Town Hall (open in holiday season) can be seen relics of the town's past, and centuries-old records. The sea used to come up to the edge of Brading and until 1594 the quay lay alongside the present High Street. For the next 300 years it was situated at the far end of Quay Lane and if you wish to stroll the ½ mile down the lane there are signs of the old quay where the former railway embankment to St Helens was built. Halfway down the lane the present railway to Ryde is crossed and before that can be seen the old village pound at the rear of the churchyard, used for the containment of loose animals. The town supplied the Spithead ships, naval and merchant, with provisions, especially beer. Unfortunately the town ceased to be a port, due mainly to schemes to drain areas of land in the Haven and eventually silting occurred. Certainly the earliest records of its use as a quay date to the medieval period, but could well go back to Roman times. A Roman villa near to the town completes the picture of the historic King's Town of Brading. In AD897, Brading Haven was the scene of a memorable battle between Viking invaders and King Alfred the Great. King Alfred won the battle. At about the same time, ownership of the manor of Brading passed into the hands of King Alfred. In 1280, Edward I awarded the town a charter and from then on it has always been referred to as the King's town.

27 Yarbridge
The Anglers

The Anglers sets out to be a traditional friendly local pub offering food and refreshment to all. The interior is comfortable and offers a cheerful welcome to all travellers. Should your visit be on Boxing Day, join one of the teams in the annual tug of war across the nearby river – there's a 50 per cent chance of getting wet. On warm days you will find a large pleasant garden with play equipment for the children, although they will still be welcome inside. The menu is based on the serving of good quality food that is sustaining and straightforward. Specialities include lasagne and there is a range of fish dishes. On the snack side, there are hearty sandwiches and ploughman's as well as a jumbo sausage in a fresh crusty roll to tempt you! This is a Gale's pub and offers Best Bitter, HSB and BBB. If you like cider try the Dry Blackthorn. Winter opening times are 10.30 am to 3 pm and 6.30 pm to 11 pm, open all day in summer. Usual Sunday restrictions apply.
Telephone: 0983 406212.

How to get there: Yarbridge is on the A3055 Sandown to Ryde road before Brading when travelling from Sandown but has no signs indicating it. Turn right at the traffic lights at the crossroads for

Bembridge (B3395) and the pub is then immediately on the right. Southern Vectis buses 16, 16B, 7 and 7A from Ventnor, Shanklin, Sandown and Ryde. Train from Shanklin, Sandown and Ryde to Brading and the walk passes the station.

Parking: The large pub car park can be used by customers while they are walking.

Length of the walk: 5 miles.

A longish walk across the river flatlands with a short sharp climb to the top of Culver, where the views are spectacular. The flatlands are of historical interest.

The Walk
Leave the pub car park and turn right down the road. Cross the bridge over the railway line and immediately turn left down steps at the side of the bridge, fingerposted public footpath. Follow the path along the wire fence. The railway is the Ryde to Shanklin electrified line and on the right is the river Yar. Approaching the station the path turns left over the line but there is a proposal for a new route here.

The new route, when established, will continue forward on the same side of the railway and pass through a disused part of the station which will be a picnic area, on the site of former platforms and lines used as the Bembridge branch. On leaving the station environs the route will continue forward to a path junction and turn right away from the line. Here the present path recrosses the line. The change will enable both crossings to be replaced by a single one nearer the station.

However, until this is all complete, turn left over the line crossing and then immediately right over a stile and follow the other side of the railway. After a few yards the path curves left to a path junction. Turn right to pass the side of gardens and cottages and exit onto a road near the station opposite the telephone box.

Turn left along the road and cross over. After about 30 yards turn right down a concrete way between the houses. A brown fingerarm points with local circular walk numbers 1 and 2. In the next cul-de-sac go forward along the road and after some 30 yards turn right again on a concrete path between houses with brown fingerarm. Pass through a metal gate to recross the railway and go down the opposite bank through a metal gate into the field – brown fingerarm number 2. Walk across the middle of the field slightly left towards a river bridge.

It is interesting whilst in this area to consider the origins of this flat land. Looking to the right, in the distance can be seen the edge of Sandown and a large squarish chapel. This flatland was open to the sea near Sandown fort, right through past Brading and to the sea at

113

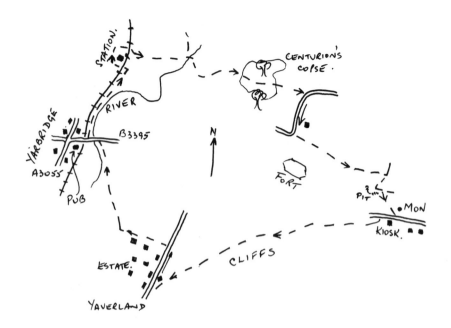

Bembridge. Thus the high ground in front of Yaverland and Culver formed an island, approachable at lower tides. A successful attempt at connecting the island to the main part of the Isle of Wight was made in the 14th century at Yarbridge. Preventing the tide running right round Bembridge inevitably caused silting up and large areas towards Sandown were reclaimed. The silting also meant that Brading was no longer suitable as a harbour – thus encouraging more attempts at reclamation.

Walk across to the bridge and note the path from the left on top of the earth wall. Turn right across the bridge and follow the top of the bank. These banks were built in the late 1500s as part of the drainage scheme, along with the sluices which can be seen under the bridges.

Continue along the embankment with views of Bembridge Down and Fort in front. Cross the stile and bridge. The path curves left with a junction to the right which is ignored. Follow the left branch winding by marshes in ancient undergrowth. Note the difference between the marshes to the left and right; probably those on the right do not have much water movement. The path rises slightly in an open area then through a blackthorn thicket to a junction. Turn right – fingerpost Culver Down.

At the next junction turn right towards Centurion's Copse and Hill. Pass through a beech copse on a wide path and at the far side of the

114

copse the path curves right, with open fields on the outside left. Go forward uphill on a slightly sunken way, which may well have been an old packhorse route, to exit on the road. Turn right along the road past the farm until the road curves sharply right. Here turn left – fingerpost Peacock Hill, Whitecliff Bay – to follow a pleasant track arched with beech. To the left can be seen Bembridge Windmill and harbour. The track turns left and right and then becomes tarmac surfaced. When it curves left with a gateway and stile on the right, cross the stile – fingerpost Culver Down – and continue across the field to the metal gate opposite. Cross a stile with a disused pit in front, go forward a few yards and then bear left steeply up on the track. After about 150 yards on the track leave it and go straight over to the monument which appears, half right. From here the views of the mainland are extensive and on a clear day the coastline towards Brighton is visible.

Leave the field by the iron gate into the lane and, with luck, the kiosk will be open for welcome refreshment. Turn right along to the cattle grid and after crossing bear left – fingerpost Sandown. Head gently away from the lane, passing to the left of the gate that isn't. Proceed downhill, parallel to the cliff edge fence, to follow the path over a sharp green bank drop to the downs below. Continue downhill getting closer to the cliff edge and then further again on a distinct path. Keep a straight line and pass between two old metal posts. The path then curves slightly right to a gate by a wind blown hedge.

In front the view is across to St Boniface and Luccombe Down with Sandown and Shanklin in the bay below. Go through the gate and forward on a worn path close to the fence. Past the holiday camp continue down into the car park, walking through it to bear right to the road by the toilets. Cross over and turn right along the road. Beware of traffic after the pavement ends. A few yards past the right turn to Sandown Bay Holiday Centre turn left up the track – fingerpost Yarbridge – and cross the stile into the field. Keep to the left edge behind the bungalows until the fence becomes a slight hedge. Here is a fingerpost to Brading, pointing right. Turn across the grass to the large oak tree with a stile beneath.

Continue in the same direction across the next field to a stile at the side of galvanised water troughs. Cross two stiles and a footbridge and continue forward to pass under the electricity wires midway between poles. Keep parallel to woodland on the right. Stray too far left and the river is in the way. There is a rail fence in front with a bridge and stile. In the next field bear left to follow the line of the river to a wooden fence and stile by the bridge. The path exits onto the road, along which turn left for the pub.

Lake
The Old Manor House

The Old Manor House is a welcoming 'town' pub. There is plenty of seating in the many rooms and in summer a small garden and patio offer a sunshine seat. In winter there is a log fire. The Old Manor House is open from 11 am to 3 pm and 7 pm to 11 pm plus all day Saturday, in winter. In summer the hours are 11 am to 11 pm, restricted on Sundays throughout the year. The real ale is Bass – always a good pint – joined in summer by others such as Tetley, Webster's or Marston's Pedigree. Blackthorn Dry is available for the cider drinker. The menu offers a choice of grills as well as doner kebab, fish dishes, steak and kidney pie and vegetarian dishes. There are several salads, plus ploughman's and sandwiches from fresh baked bread. In summer there is a roast on every day (in winter on Sundays only) and daily board specials. Children are very welcome in the family room. Dogs may be brought in – but only if well behaved. Bed and breakfast accommodation is also available.

Telephone: 0983 403558.

How to get there: Lake lies between Shanklin and Sandown and the pub fronts onto the main road between the railway bridge and the war memorial. Southern Vectis bus nos 2, 3, 16, 16B, 7 and 7A from

Sandown, Shanklin, Ryde and Newport. If you arrive by British Rail turn left from the station, walk for ½ mile and turn left. Walk under the railway bridge and the pub is on your right.

Parking: There is a small rear car park where a vehicle may be left during a walk. Please note that the area in front of the pub is a garage forecourt – not a car park. There is also some street parking.

Length of the walk: 4 miles.

This is an easily accessed and remarkably rural walk. An extremely pleasant mile follows a stream valley and the route returns along the cliffs.

The Walk

From the Old Manor House turn right along the main road towards the war memorial. Turn almost immediately right into Lake Green Road, passing two petrol stations. Continue along the length of this road passing a turning to the left. At the end the grassy start of Lake Common opens up and the walk continues along the rough track on the left borders of the common. At the end of the track bear left up a path – fingerpost Borthwood. Go through the kissing gate and when the path divides in a few yards, take the left track through the copse and out to the golf course. Cross the course but beware of flying balls. The path passes between a large scrub area on the right and a small collection of newly planted trees on the left. On the far side can just be seen the back of a notice board in the bushes. Views to the right are of Brading and Ashey Down with the white sea mark on top.

At the board the path goes forward through a small copse to a stile above a track, which you cross slightly right to another stile. Go down the steps and bear slightly right again to a footbridge. Across the field make for a sturdy bridge and a rail fence into a spinney. Cross the stile and when through the spinney, the buildings of Sandown Airport can be seen in front. In this next field turn sharp left and follow the left edge with the spinney on the left. Continue to follow the edge round. Behind a mesh fence can be seen a private lake. Follow the left edge along until the field narrows to a strip before opening up to a huge field. Cross to the right over this strip. Usually there is a trodden path somewhere in the narrow area. The path is now on the right edge of the field with the wire fence of the airfield on the right. Continue to the end and cross the stile in the corner, fingerposted public footpath. Continue forward along a wide grassy strip with a spinney to the left and the grass runway to the right. This is a good section from which to observe the aircraft movement. Although only a grass runway the airfield is used a lot for private and pleasure flights and in the summer

117

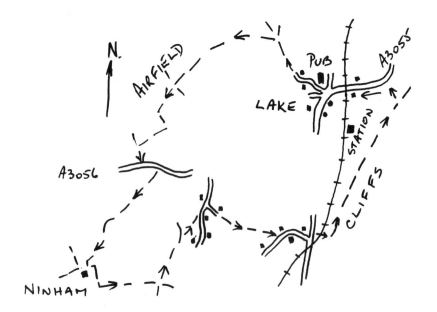

can be very busy. At the end of the grassy strip note the fingerpost pointing right. This is an unusual path in that it passes completely across the runway, but good visibility has meant no conflict between foot and flight and the path across is a very popular local walk.

However, the route turns left towards a stile at the next fingerpost. Do not cross the stile but turn right, still along the edge of the airfield. No fingerarm points this direction, but go forward with the hedge and ditch on the left and a wire fence on the right, heading towards the hangars and parking aprons. At the end of this straight grass strip turn left, fingerposted public footpath. Walk along the edge which is now a gravel perimeter track. This swings right by some dismantled old aircraft and passes to the left of a building. By the electricity poles and transformer is a public footpath sign. Bear slightly right towards a green building and the fir trees. Cut across to the corner of the trees and then go along the edge with a line of trees on the left and at the end join the main drive by a fingerpost. Turn left down the drive and then left down the main road. After about 100 yards pause on the bridge with white rails over a stream. Across the road at the right end of the rails is a small gap. Pass through and drop into the grass below – fingerpost Ninham, Scotchells Brook. Cross the footbridge and go forward along the stream edge. The path swings slightly right away from the stream and then gradually rejoins it. This is a delightful strip of old undisturbed wetlands. The path winds forward, generally close to the stream on the left, the full length of the strip, which widens a little and then narrows again. Go forward with the stream always a few yards to the left and cross the sidestreams over simple plank bridges.

On the map is marked Ninham withy beds, where twigs were collected from willow or reeds and used for basket making or thatching. At the end pass through a metal gate and go forward to a fingerpost. Turn left along a track over the stream and between two private farm ponds. Ducks and geese abound as do daffodils in spring. At the next gate pass through the zigzag on the right and bear left along the tarmac track. At the next corner turn right – fingerpost Landguard. Walk along the track which curves left by a caravan park, then down through bends to reach a crossroads of tracks by woodland. Views to the right are of Shanklin Down and left is our old friend Ashey sea mark. Turn left, fingerposted Old Highway, Scotchells.

Go forward along the track which connects two main roads, Newport/Sandown and Newport/Shanklin, and was probably the original cart road through the farms of Landguard, Lower Hyde and Upper Hyde before the coast road was built. Cross the stile by the metal gate and over the stream on a stone bridge. Bear right off the track to the stile and steps, fingerpost Landguard, Whitecross. In the field bear half left up the slope and over the crest. Ahead can be seen a fingerpost and stile. Cross into the road and turn left along it. Turn right at the second turning (the first is a tiny close) opposite the cottages. Walk along the road, then the concrete track and at the end follow the narrow sunken path uphill. Go over the top and down to exit on a tarmac close. I find back gardens most interesting.

Go down the close and turn left into Green Lane which curves right as Cemetery Road. Cross the main road to walk up a gravel drive between properties. Go through two white gates protecting the railway line (take care crossing) and the cliff top area is reached. Go forward on a tarmac path to the cliff edge and turn left along the cliff top walk. Views ahead are across Sandown pier to Culver Cliff with the monument on top and to the rear can be seen Shanklin esplanade and Luccombe Down behind. The cliff path becomes a back road and then a cliff path again.

At this point a telephone box is on the left. Walk a few yards and turn left on a broad tarmac path between stone walls. Continue with the old battery on the right to pass into a cul-de-sac and out onto the main road opposite the Leisure Centre. Turn left down the hill, under the railway to return to the Old Manor House.

St Helens
The Vine Inn

St Helens is known for its bonfire society who meet each year to arrange the celebrations, which are always on 5th November. The original society, formed some 50 years ago, met in the cellar of the Vine Inn. The visitor who has a liking for unusual foods is advised to make the inn a stopping place, as well as those who enjoy a pint in a village pub. The Vine was built around 300 years ago as a pub to provide refreshment for the workers at the nearby harbour. A solid plain building, it has had no great historical events occurring under its roof, yet it has outlived the numerous other pubs in St Helens. In the garden can be found a headstone dated 1911 in memory of Whisky – not the drink but a previous landlord's very old dog. The landlord apparently closed the pub on every anniversary, such was his attachment to his friend.

Inside, the inn has a village pub atmosphere and serves pub food, being particularly known for steak and kidney pie, lasagne and ocean pie. However an unusual menu in a foreign language will be found on the bar. The landlord's wife specialises in genuine Thai food, having originated from those parts, and is herself the chef. A separate building at the rear is an à la carte Thai restaurant, open evenings only, booking necessary. Some of the items, however, are available as bar food and 'take away' is also on the menu. The liquid refreshments are less exotic perhaps, but include some of local origin. Real ales from the island – Caulkhead and in the summer Newport Bitter – provide a good pint, Flowers IPA and Marston's Pedigree offering a further choice. If you are a cider drinker Scrumpy Jack is available. There is a small beer garden for summer use and children are accommodated in the back of the lounge before 8.30 pm. Should you have a dog with you he is welcome but beware the ghost of Whisky.

The opening times are 11 am to 3 pm and 6.30 pm to 11 pm each day, increasing to 11 am to 11 pm with holiday times, July and August. Sunday opening is the usual restricted times.

Telephone: 0983 872337.

How to get there: St Helens is on the coast road from Ryde through Nettlestone to Bembridge but is best reached from the main Ryde to Sandown road, the A3055. The turn on the B3330 is one mile north of Brading. The Vine overlooks the village green. Southern Vectis buses nos 7 and 7A from Ryde and Sandown.

Parking: There is no car park at the pub but a large free one is on the side of the green near the pub.

Length of the walk: 3 ½ miles.

The outward walk is by the sea on a newly created path just off the shore whilst the return is a stroll over grassy fields. The coastal path is reasonably strenuous and is rewarded by views across the Solent and Spithead. The route at the far end of the coastal section varies with the tide.

The Walk
From the public car park cross the lower green area and walk down Latimer Road, at the side of the St Helens Service Station. Follow the road to the bottom where it bends sharply right. Go forward a few yards and then turn sharply left into North Quay. Pass in front of the flats, Selwyn Court, and then bear left on a track at the water's edge. Turn right to follow the quay side with a stone building on the left. A plaque high on the front wall says that this was St Helens Mill, built in 1780. This was a tidal mill, powered by water retained on a high tide. Follow the stone garden wall and turn left with it. This concrete area faces water (or mud if the tide's out) with a green corrugated building on the right. Pass at the back of that building – even though it looks impossible! The narrow path runs behind, fingerposted St Helens, Duver and Seaview, and joins onto the causeway. Walk

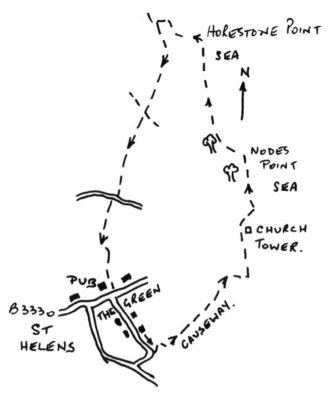

along this with a large area which was formerly the mill pond on the left. The tide ran through the causeway gaps, into which gates were dropped at high tide. The path crosses these gaps on short bridges.

At the end of the causeway, from which Bembridge and its harbour can be seen to the right, walk forward on a broad grassy area. After passing a scrub area on the right, bear slightly right towards barriers forming a car park. Cross a tarmac lane and go into the car park to the information board. A 'duver' is the local name for a narrow sandy spit, here formed by the tide sweeping across the mouth of the estuary. From the late 19th century to 1961 the Duver was occupied by the links of the Royal Isle of Wight Golf Club, of which the original club house has been preserved and lies along the lane. Now turn right and walk along the edge of the lower car park to leave by steps in the far corner. Go along the left edge of the grassy area heading for the green buildings. Turn left through the barriers and onto the sea front. Those green 'buildings' were formerly railway carriages.

Turn left along the concrete front past the café and toilets to reach the tower at the far end. This tower, built in the reign of Henry III, is all that remains of St Helens church which began to crumble into the sea in 1550. It was bricked up on the seaward side in 1703 and whitened to act as a sea mark. It is said sailors removed the old stones for use on board to rub and clean the decks, from which the term 'holystoning' originated.

Continue along the sea wall to enter the National Trust area, Nodes Point. At the end of the sea wall continue along the beach edge for some 60 yards in a tiny bay. The path starts on the left at a waymark and passes up a few steps into scrubland. It then curves to the right and up further steps to contour along above the shore. Continue on a man-made shelf through scrubland. The way twists and turns, rises and falls, but there is always a distinct main path. Avoid all side paths running to the beach. The sea can be seen below right, whilst a low cliff rises on the left. The path passes through rough woodland. Go forward on a path crossing a short boardwalk area. Further on cross a plank bridge followed by two sections of boardwalk then a small boardwalk bridge followed by a flight of steps. Go through a slightly more open area with a wider view onto the beach and then bear left sharply up steps to the top of the bluff. Go over the top and down steps.

The beach to the right is now a different bay. Pass over a series of short boardwalks, winding along somewhat higher from the beach. A longish boardwalk through the trees brings the path past a notice 'Priory Woods'. Go along the path with remnants of a metal fence on the left. The route eventually turns sharply left through the fence and up a flight of steps. At the top bear right on a narrow path through a bramble area, then through the trees with a field and buildings visible across to the left. Curve slightly right on the path to arrive at the top of a flight of stairs down to the beach. At the beach turn left along the sea wall – note an old pumping engine on the left. Walk along to the boathouse and perhaps rest awhile to look out to sea. To the far right can be seen the Bembridge lifeboat house and on the horizon to the left of the lifeboat the Nab Tower is just visible. Moving further left, St Helen's fort is close in with the Spithead forts, built by Palmerston as defences against French invasion, further left still. The mainland can be seen on the left horizon running away east towards Bognor Regis.

Continue along the shingle past the boathouse for about 50 yards. The rocks of Horestone Point approach in the sea. The steps leading left off the shore to the top of the point are useful at high tide. If the tide is down walk round the point on the shore, an easier route. Walk up the steps and bear slightly right, not straight on. Cross the top of the point and go sharply down into a tiny inlet with broken concrete blocks to reach the shore again and rejoin the beach route round the point. From here the path is on the shore all the way along to a white painted café/shop with a slipway at the bottom of a lane. However, at various states of the tide different routes are used and there is a slight path on the shore side of the timber stakes. The esplanade is private but is always well used by the general public.

Turn left up the lane past public conveniences, Furnclose Road – fingerpost St Helens, Duver and Bembridge. Go forward uphill ignoring the junction to the right. Continue on a rough track uphill past exclusive properties. At the far end, at a junction keep forward to enter a path. In a few yards ignore the path going left but cross the stile ahead. Follow the left edge of the grass fields with a hedge on the left. There are views to the left of Culver Down and monument and to the right over the inland downs. Go forward to the road at a metal kissing gate and turn right. A few yards along the road turn left – fingerpost St Helens – into an enclosed path with a fence on the right. At the end of the caravan site on the right continue forward at the junction between houses, cross an estate road and follow the path forward to walk down the side of the Vine Inn.

㉚ Bembridge
The Crab and Lobster

Despite its popularity this pub is probably one of the most difficult to find. If you are walking the coastal path it comes as a welcome surprise, whilst by road it would never appear by chance. It is well worth searching for. Built in 1810 as a pub, there is a pleasant exterior at the front with a small sheltered patio and a few tables in the open providing quite a compact outdoor area, although one can sit on the low wall or alfresco on the grass. The views from here are extensive. Inside look in the alcove for the comfy armchairs and settee!

Summertime opening is 10.30 am to 3 pm and 6 pm to 11 pm whilst in wintertime they start an hour later in the morning and ½ hour later in the evening. Sunday has the standard restricted times. The menu offers a good range of homecooked food from sausage to fish, with tasty sandwiches and ploughman's for those not requiring a hot meal. There is also a range of sea food on the bar menu. At lunchtimes the dining room is also available for bar food – the only time and place for those accompanied by children. In the evening this area becomes an à la carte restaurant, but bar food remains available in other areas. The restaurant is only open from Easter to October and specialises in sea food, much of it island caught, including lobster and crab. An

extensive wine list complements the food and a mouthwatering range of sweets is available for those who still have room. On the drinks side the real ales are Flowers Original and Tetley, this one changing occasionally for other guest ales. Four barrels behind the bar offer a choice of cherry, peach, apricot or damson fruit wines.
Telephone: 0983 872244.

How to get there: The pub is at the Forelands. It is signposted, but often on small signs. Lane End is near to the Forelands so those signs can be followed first. From St Helens pass along Bembridge main street, but from Sandown it is not necessary to go to the village centre. Eventually pass Lane End shops, then turn right into Egerton Road, left at the end and immediately right into Foreland Fields Road. This lane turns left and twists down to the pub, but see 'parking' for what to do next. Southern Vectis buses nos 7 and 7A from Shanklin, Sandown and Ryde to Bembridge – restricted in winter.

Parking: The pub car park is very restricted. You may be lucky but certainly should not leave your car there while you walk. In Foreland Fields road, when the lane turns left continue forward through a gate into a large area in front of and past new properties. This is a private car park, open for general parking but you may be asked to pay. This car park is only a few yards from the pub and the walk starts here.

Length of the walk: 4 miles.

A walk which mixes coast and inland. The coastal stretches are at the water's edge and on low cliffs, whilst inland is through woodland and visits Bembridge Windmill. No strenuous uphill walking involved.

The Walk
Walk to the coastal end of the car park and leave by the small path in the left corner, slightly hidden. This narrow path under a wall exits in front of the pub. From the pub, walk in front of the coastguard station and then bear left through a gate – fingerpost Coast Path. Follow the gravel track in front of the houses and when this becomes hard-surfaced, turn right down a narrow path between houses. The house called Magnolia Lodge is on the right of the path. The path exits into a cul-de-sac. Bear half left across the green area and the road to find another path between houses numbers 23 and 21. Follow this narrow way to reach yet another cul-de-sac. Follow this road (Poplar Close) and at a road junction continue forward along a rough track (Foreland Farm Lane). About 100 yards along turn right down an enclosed path – fingerpost Coastal Path. The path runs under pine trees, crosses the

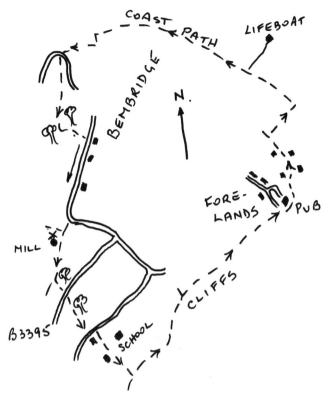

entrance road to Warners' Bembridge site and meets the coast at the
end of a grass strip.

Turn left along the grassy area at the edge of the low cliff. Look far
out on the horizon directly out to sea and on a clear day a shape similar
to a submarine conning tower can be seen. This is a construction
called the Nab Tower and was a defensive fort, now a most distinctive
sea mark. Walk to the shore end of the catwalk and continue along the
coast on the surfaced sea wall with houses and gardens on the left.

At the end of the sea wall continue forward, down and up steps and
along a narrow strip between fence and shingle bank. This is above
high water mark but at lower tides you may wish to walk along the
sand and beachcomb. Pass two green chalets/boathouses and turn left
away from the beach up a series of concrete steps. Turn right, parallel
to the coast and close under the hedge. When you reach a junction
with wooden boards in front, turn right back to the beach and left
along the beach edge, keeping up off the beach at high water.
Continue forward on a path which can be rough in places but

generally runs on the landward side of timber revetment posts.

Just before rounding the point, a red and white banded post is seen on the right protruding from the sea (or rocks at low tide). A few yards before coming level with the post a small path bears left into the lower woodland. Follow this winding path, under a huge fallen tree, parallel to the beach but in the woodland. A shallow cliff is up on the left. The way rounds the point and comes close to the beach again. Here the view seawards and forwards is across Bembridge harbour to the Duver and St Helens church (now a white sea mark). A few beach huts appear on the right of the path, which now becomes enclosed between fences and exits onto a rough track. Turn left up this away from the coast. After about 75 yards a fingerpost on the left of the track points to Bembridge Point to the right. Turn right between houses. The path becomes a track and exits onto the road at the Point.

The route crosses the road into the lane past public toilets and the Row Barge Inn. Pass to the side of high wire enclosing tennis courts and bear slightly right. The path runs along the edge of a marshy area with an iron fence to the left. Beware the slippery timbers underfoot! At the end of this section the path curves left uphill (ignore a side path to the right) to exit onto the road.

Turn right along the road using the pavement for a while. When the road turns sharp left continue forward down a gravel track to Bembridge Windmill. The last remaining windmill on the Island, it has stood since about 1700, and ground cereals until 1913; it is open at times and visitors can examine the original machinery. Continue forward with the mill on the right down the track – fingerpost Steyne Wood. In front can be seen Culver Down with its distinctive memorial. The way enters the edge of woodland. After a few yards turn left onto a footpath leaving the straight bridleway. Follow this path to the road, cross carefully and continue uphill slightly, in woodland. Exit onto the next road at a stile and turn left up the road.

Partway up the slope turn right onto a tarmac track marked 'public footpath'. Walk along this through a copse and then into a green area with a large green corrugated building on the right. Continue forward and across the lane, fingerposted public footpath, to reach another fingerpost. This points down the side of a recreation field under a line of evergreens. Follow this path to the coast path. The buildings of Bembridge School are to the left.

Turn left along the coast path, outside the playing field. The path eventually skirts the edge of the field and at the end bears right – fingerpost Coastal Path. Continue along this and at the next junction turn right to reach the parking area with a free-range animal farm on the left.